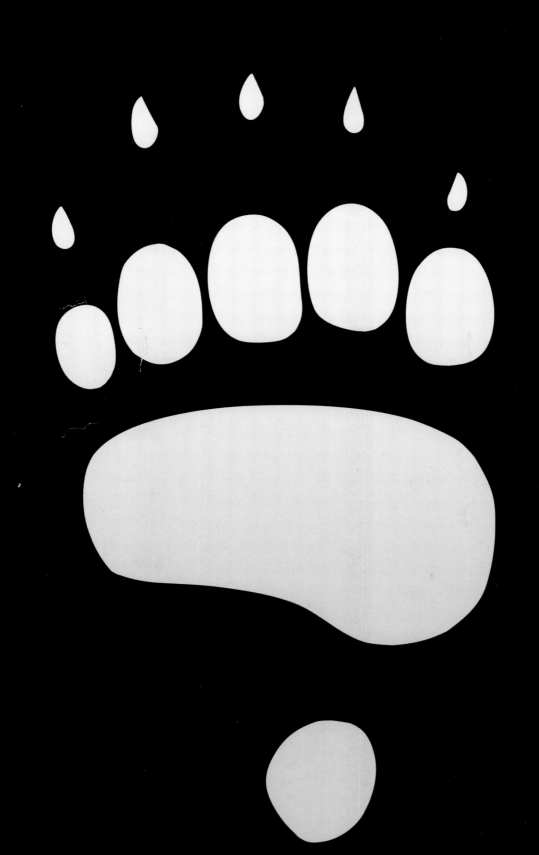

BEARS

WRITTEN & ILLUSTRATED BY
TED RECHLIN

PRESENTED BY

REXTOOTH STUDIOS

EDITOR
ANNE RECHLIN

BEARS

COPYRIGHT © 2016 BY TED RECHLIN

PUBLISHED BY REXTOOTH STUDIOS, BOZEMAN, MONTANA

PRODUCED BY SWEETGRASS BOOKS, HELENA, MONTANA

ISBN 13: 978-1-59152-186-0

COVER DESIGN BY TED RECHLIN

PRODUCED IN THE UNITED STATES OF AMERICA

PRINTED IN CHINA

For the bears.

They make the wilderness wild.

GRIZZLY BEAR

URSUS ARCTOS

THE ROCKY MOUNTAINS

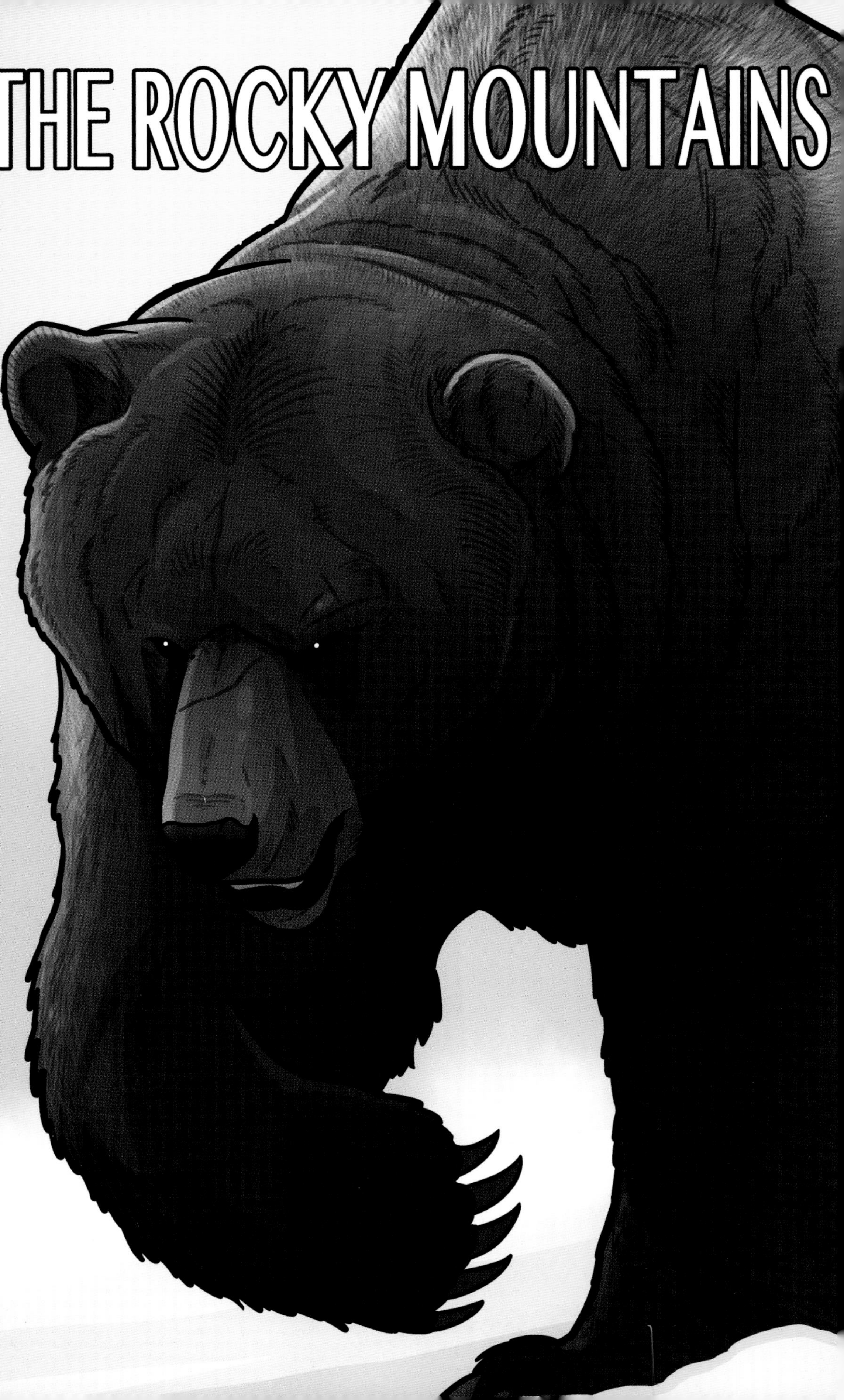

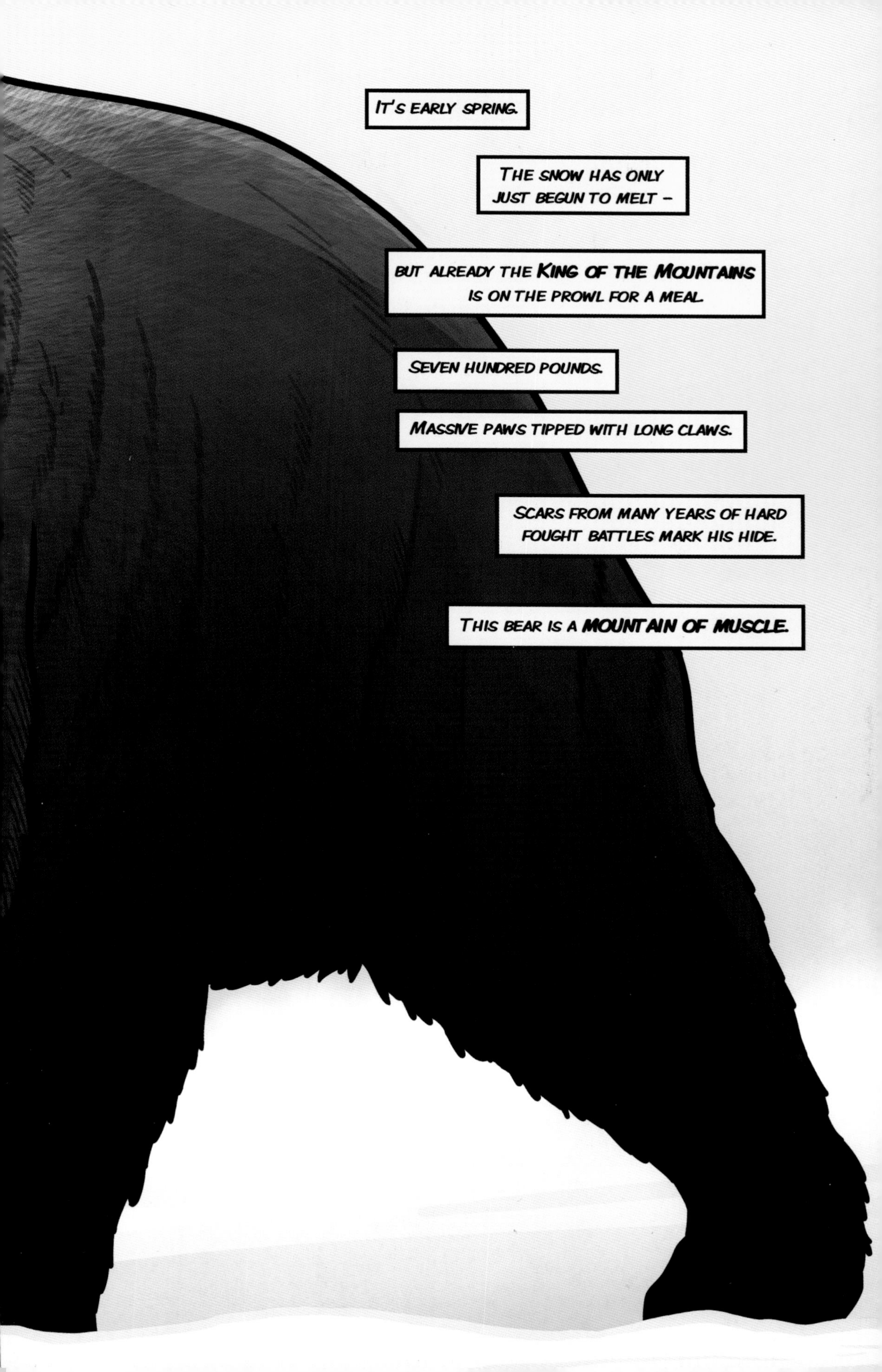
IT'S EARLY SPRING.
THE SNOW HAS ONLY JUST BEGUN TO MELT –
BUT ALREADY THE KING OF THE MOUNTAINS IS ON THE PROWL FOR A MEAL.
SEVEN HUNDRED POUNDS.
MASSIVE PAWS TIPPED WITH LONG CLAWS.
SCARS FROM MANY YEARS OF HARD FOUGHT BATTLES MARK HIS HIDE.
THIS BEAR IS A MOUNTAIN OF MUSCLE.

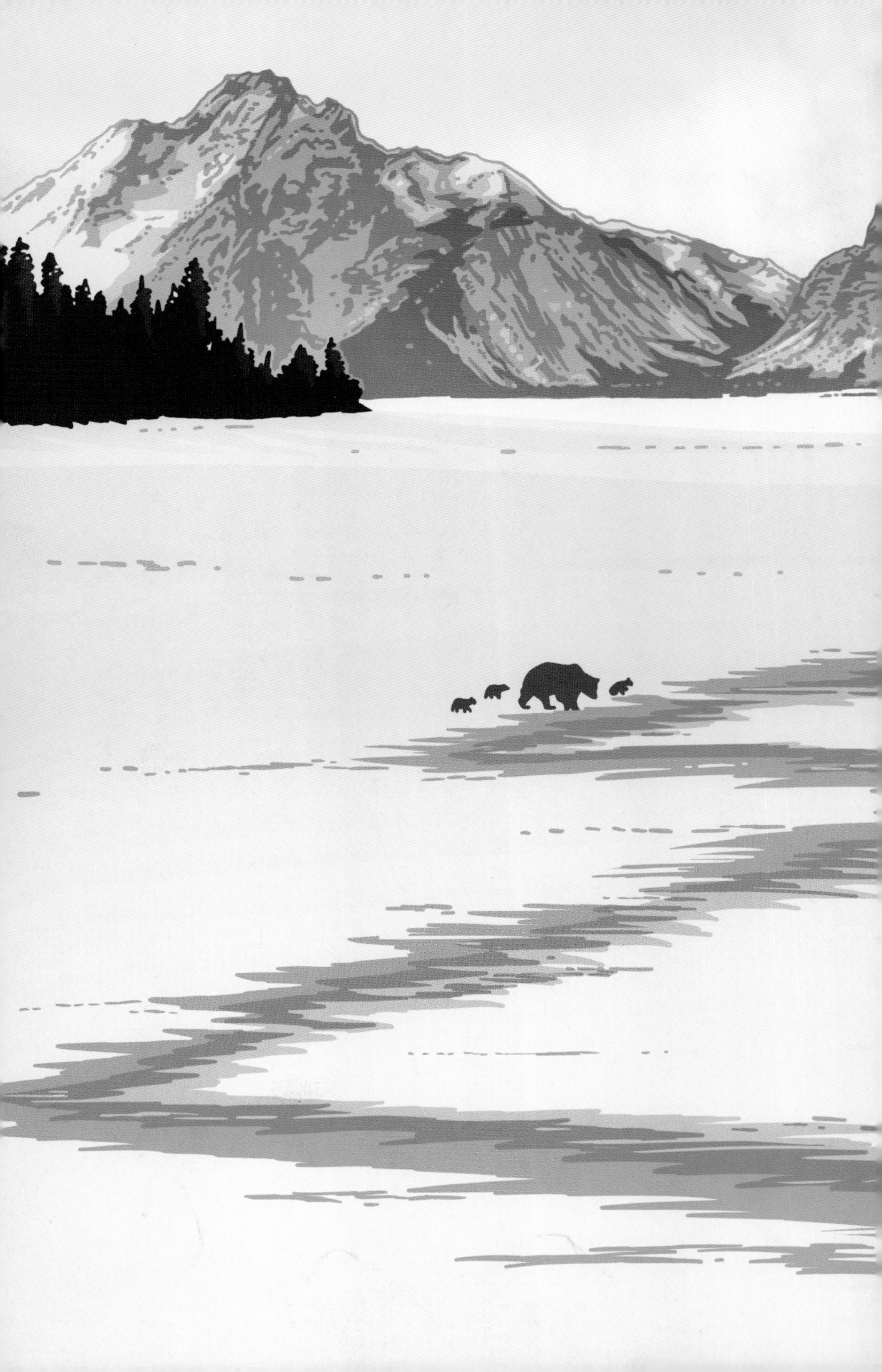

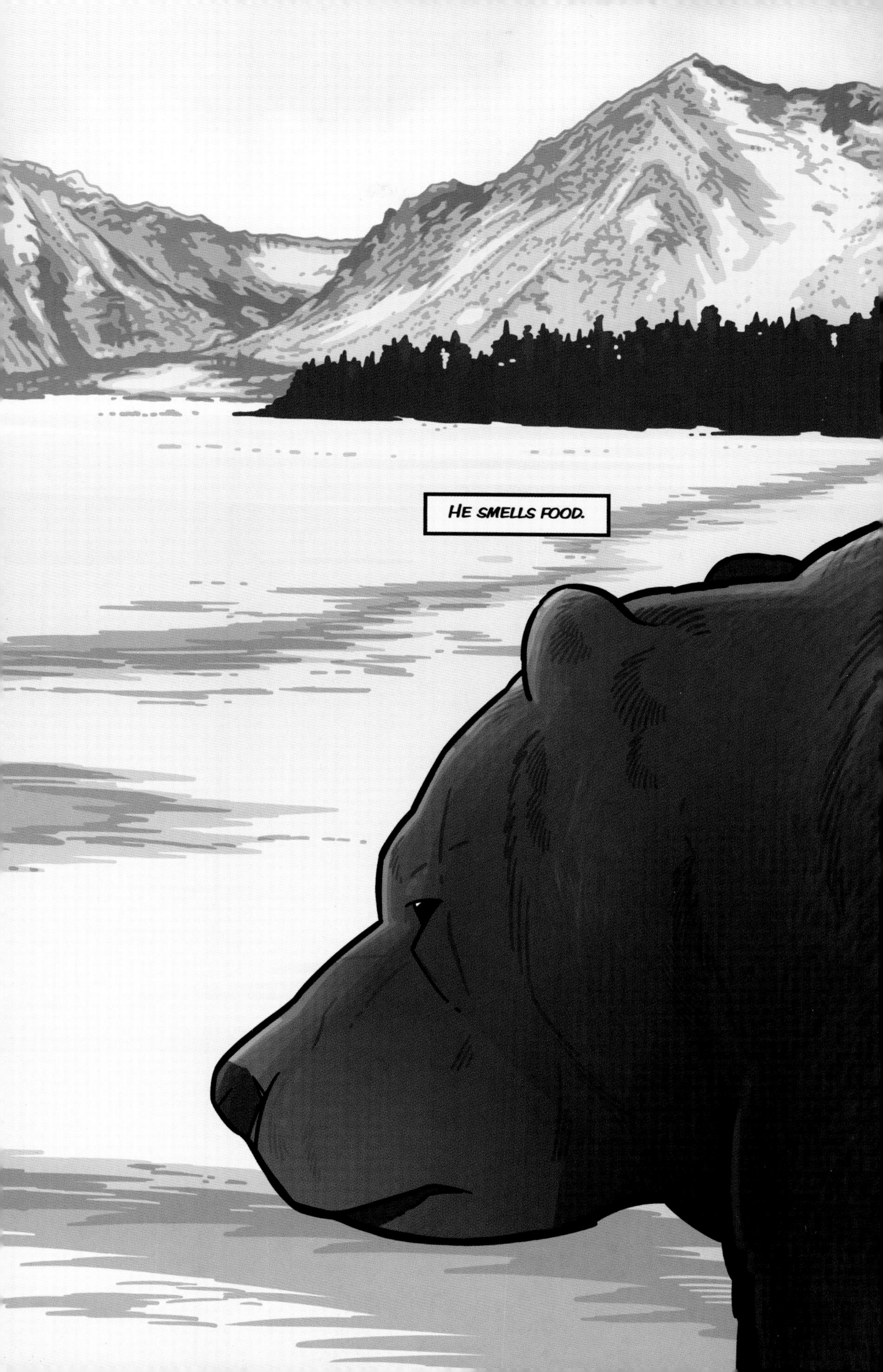
HE SMELLS FOOD.

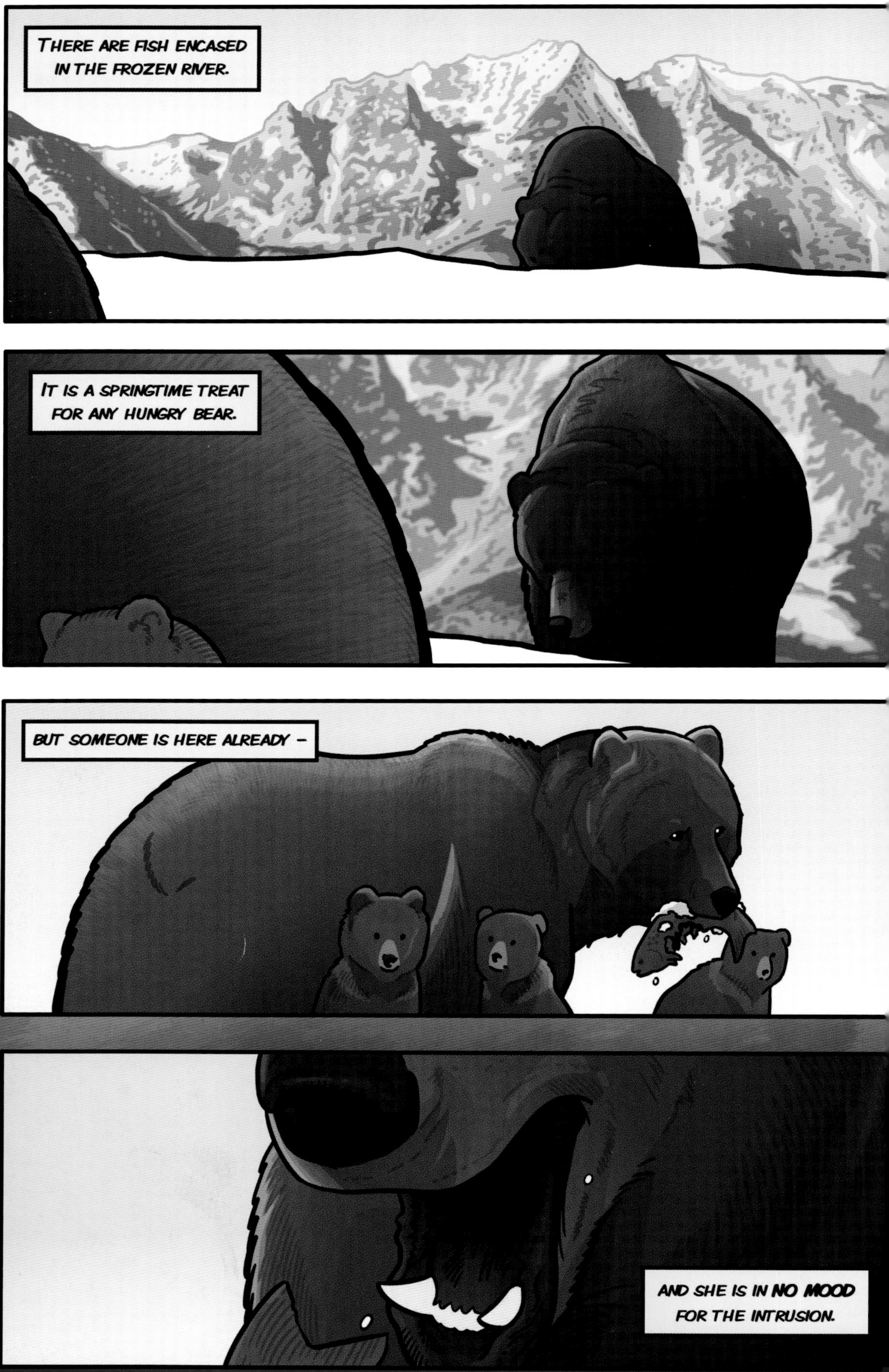
THERE ARE FISH ENCASED IN THE FROZEN RIVER.
IT IS A SPRINGTIME TREAT FOR ANY HUNGRY BEAR.
BUT SOMEONE IS HERE ALREADY –
AND SHE IS IN NO MOOD FOR THE INTRUSION.

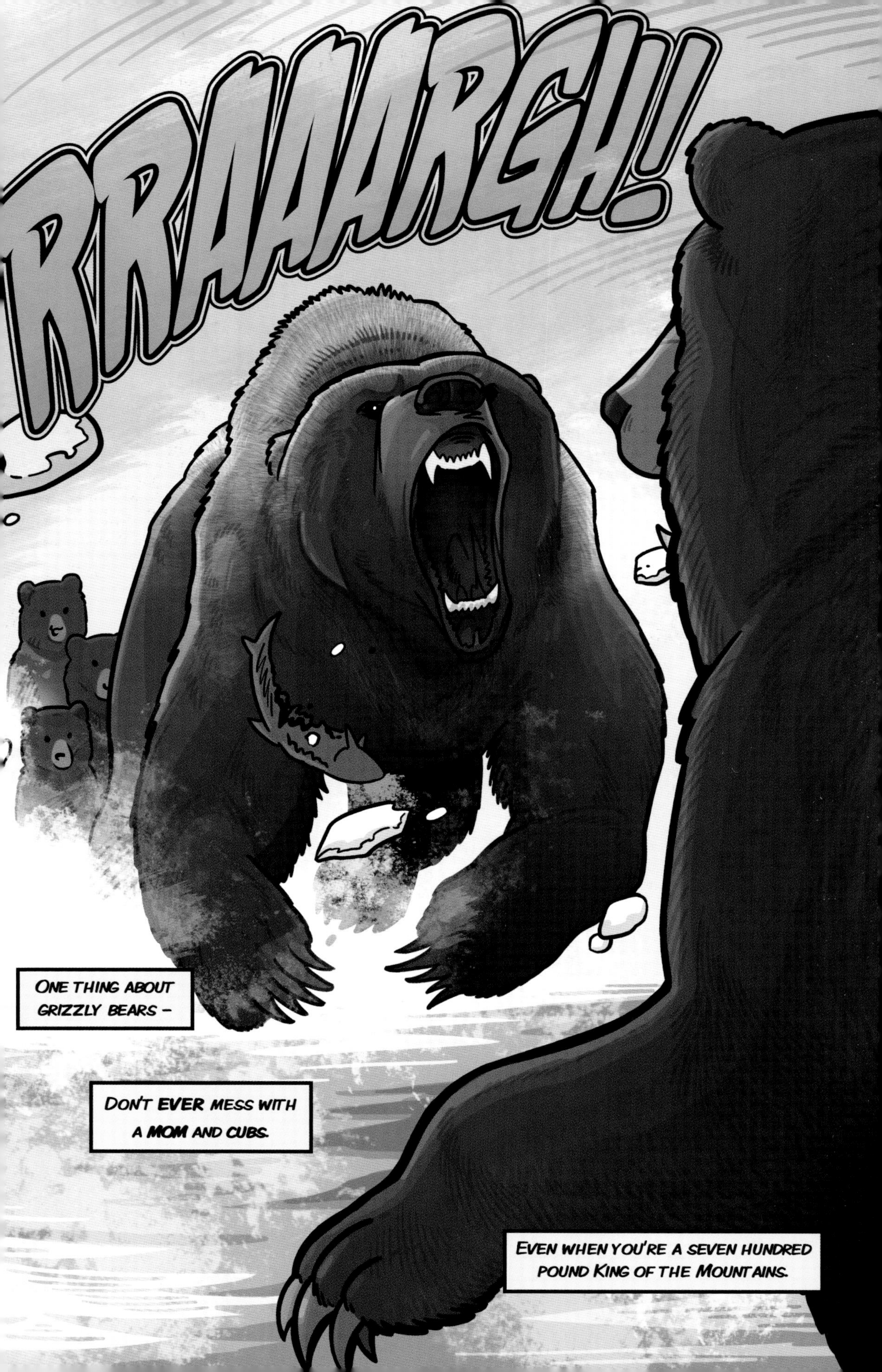
RRAAARGH!!
ONE THING ABOUT GRIZZLY BEARS –
DON'T EVER MESS WITH A MOM AND CUBS.
EVEN WHEN YOU'RE A SEVEN HUNDRED POUND KING OF THE MOUNTAINS.

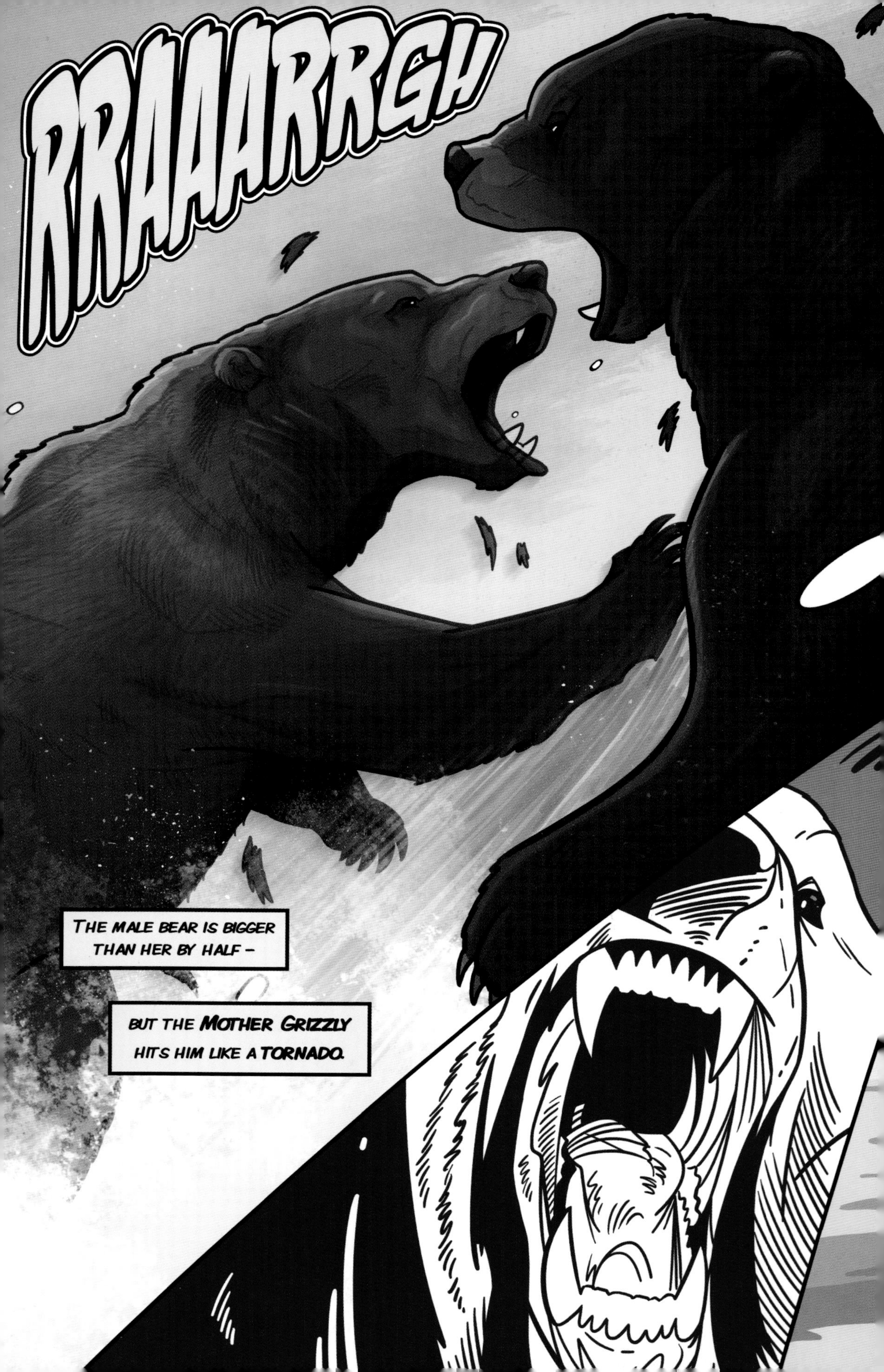
RRAAARRRGH
THE MALE BEAR IS BIGGER THAN HER BY HALF –
BUT THE MOTHER GRIZZLY HITS HIM LIKE A TORNADO.

HE MAY HAVE ONLY COME TO THE RIVER LOOKING FOR FISH –
BUT MALE BEARS WILL **KILL** TINY CUBS LIKE THESE.
CHOMP
SO THIS MOM **CAN'T** AFFORD TO TAKE ANY CHANCES.
RRGH!
SHE SENDS HIM PACKING WITH A FEW NEW SCARS –
AND A BRUISED EGO.

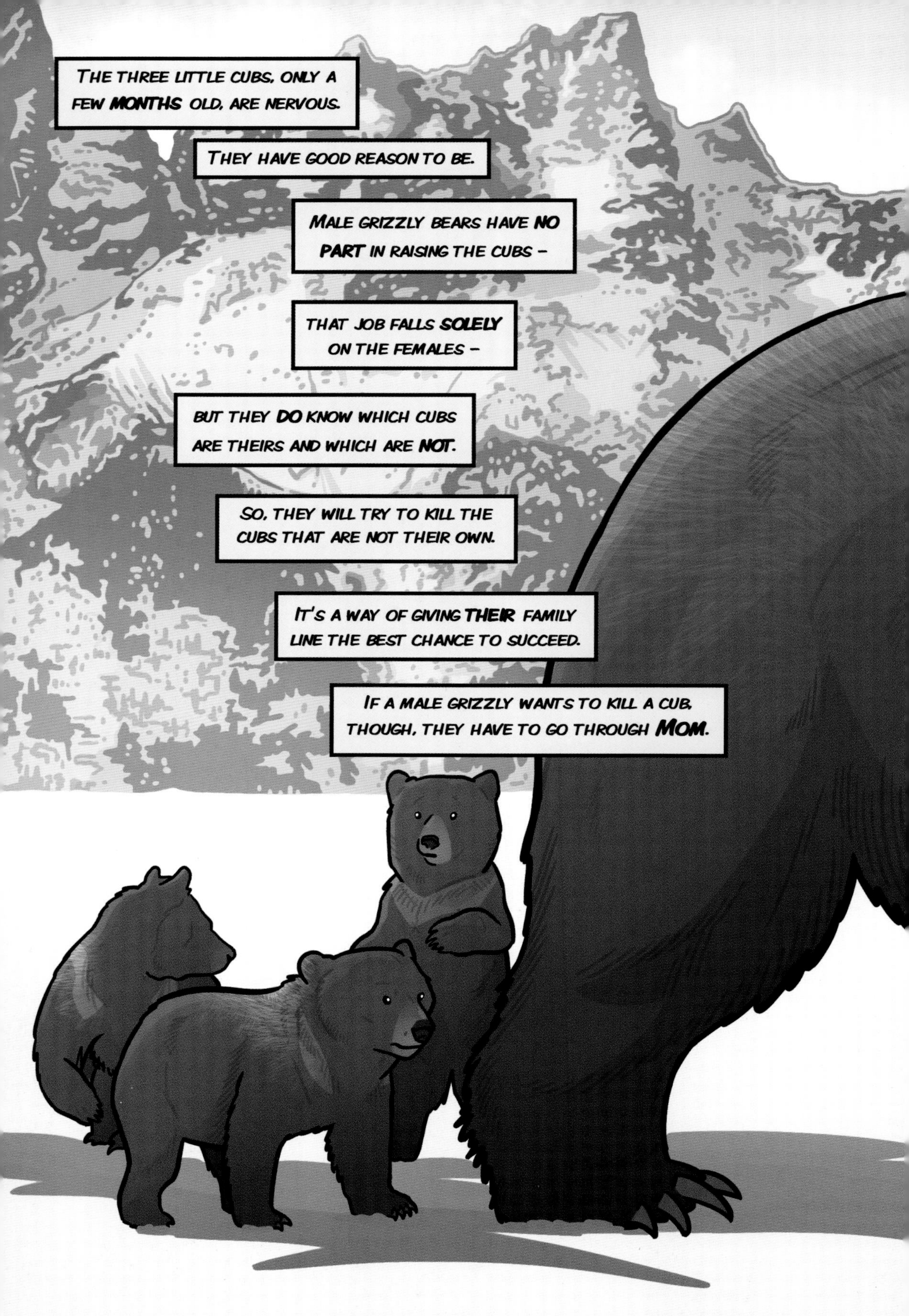
THE THREE LITTLE CUBS, ONLY A FEW MONTHS OLD, ARE NERVOUS.
THEY HAVE GOOD REASON TO BE.
MALE GRIZZLY BEARS HAVE NO PART IN RAISING THE CUBS –
THAT JOB FALLS SOLELY ON THE FEMALES –
BUT THEY DO KNOW WHICH CUBS ARE THEIRS AND WHICH ARE NOT.
SO, THEY WILL TRY TO KILL THE CUBS THAT ARE NOT THEIR OWN.
IT'S A WAY OF GIVING THEIR FAMILY LINE THE BEST CHANCE TO SUCCEED.
IF A MALE GRIZZLY WANTS TO KILL A CUB, THOUGH, THEY HAVE TO GO THROUGH MOM.

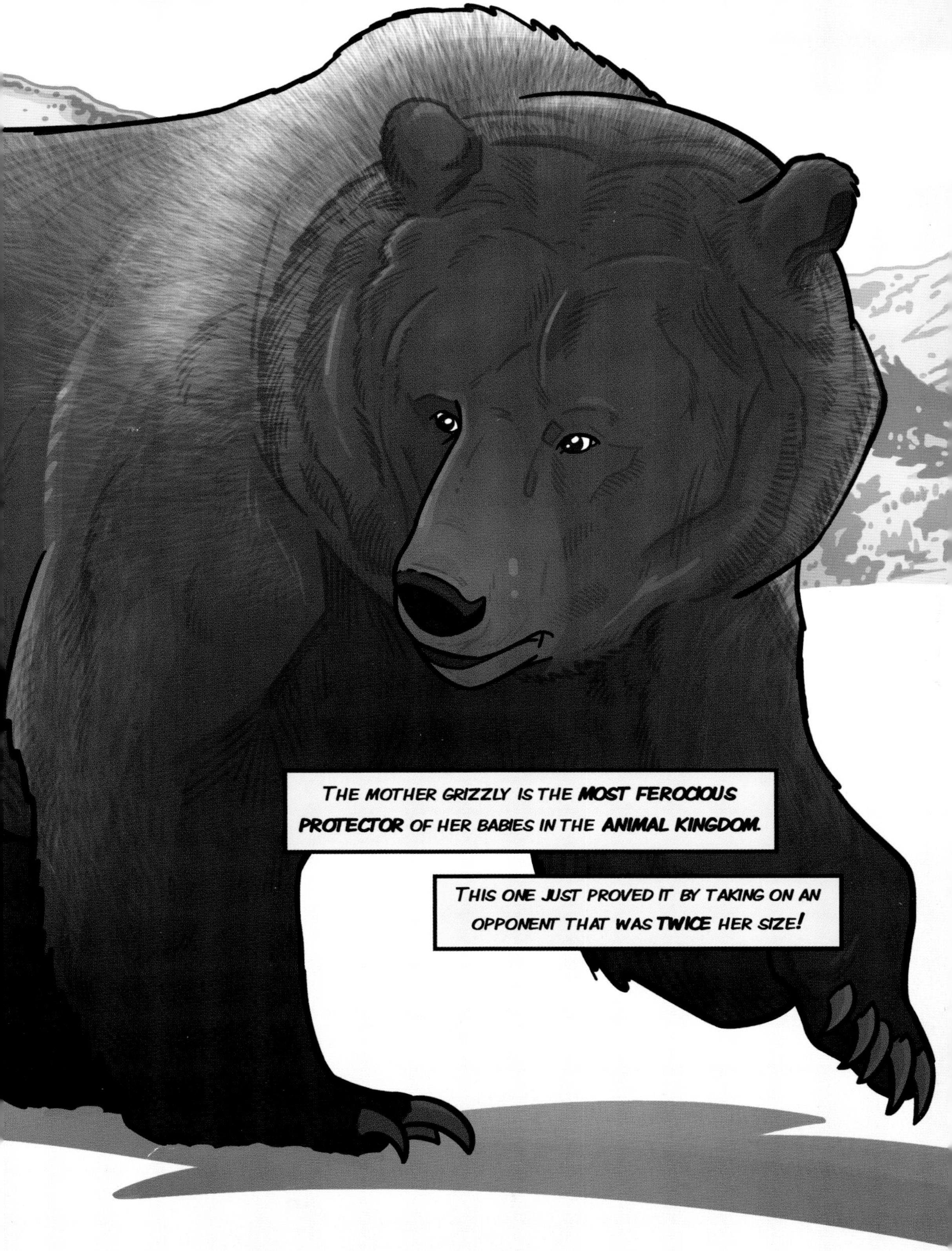
THE MOTHER GRIZZLY IS THE MOST FEROCIOUS PROTECTOR OF HER BABIES IN THE ANIMAL KINGDOM.
THIS ONE JUST PROVED IT BY TAKING ON AN OPPONENT THAT WAS TWICE HER SIZE!

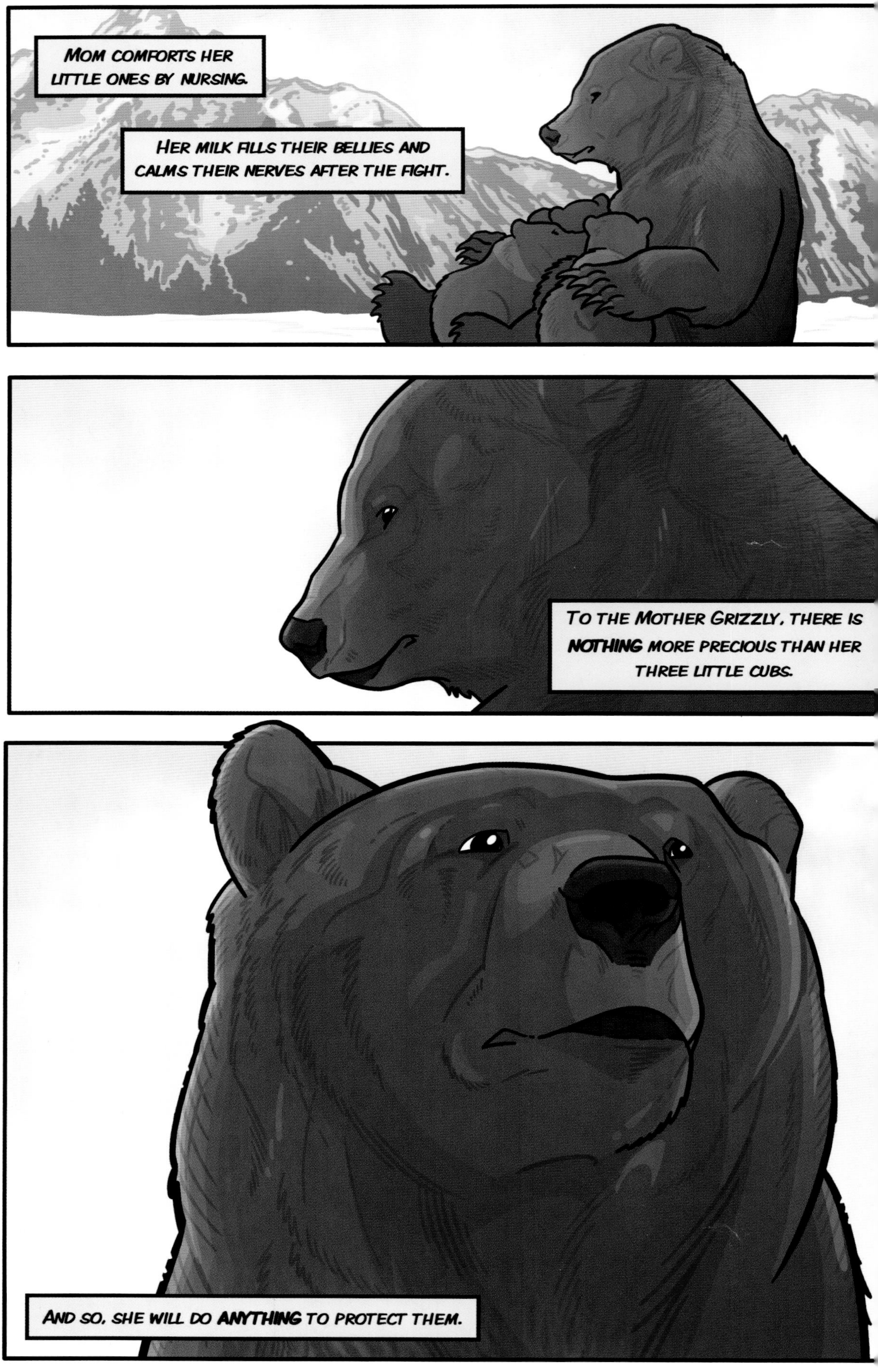
MOM COMFORTS HER LITTLE ONES BY NURSING.
HER MILK FILLS THEIR BELLIES AND CALMS THEIR NERVES AFTER THE FIGHT.
TO THE MOTHER GRIZZLY, THERE IS NOTHING MORE PRECIOUS THAN HER THREE LITTLE CUBS.
AND SO, SHE WILL DO ANYTHING TO PROTECT THEM.

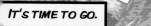
IT'S TIME TO GO.

THE ROCKY MOUNTAIN BACKCOUNTRY, AND ITS **BOUNTY** OF FOOD AND SPACE, IS THE PERFECT BEAR HABITAT.

BUT THIS MOM **KNOWS** SHE AND HER CUBS **CANNOT** STAY HERE.

THE BIG MALE BEAR COULD COME BACK.

AND SHE WON'T RISK HER CUBS SAFETY.

SO IT'S TIME TO **GO.**

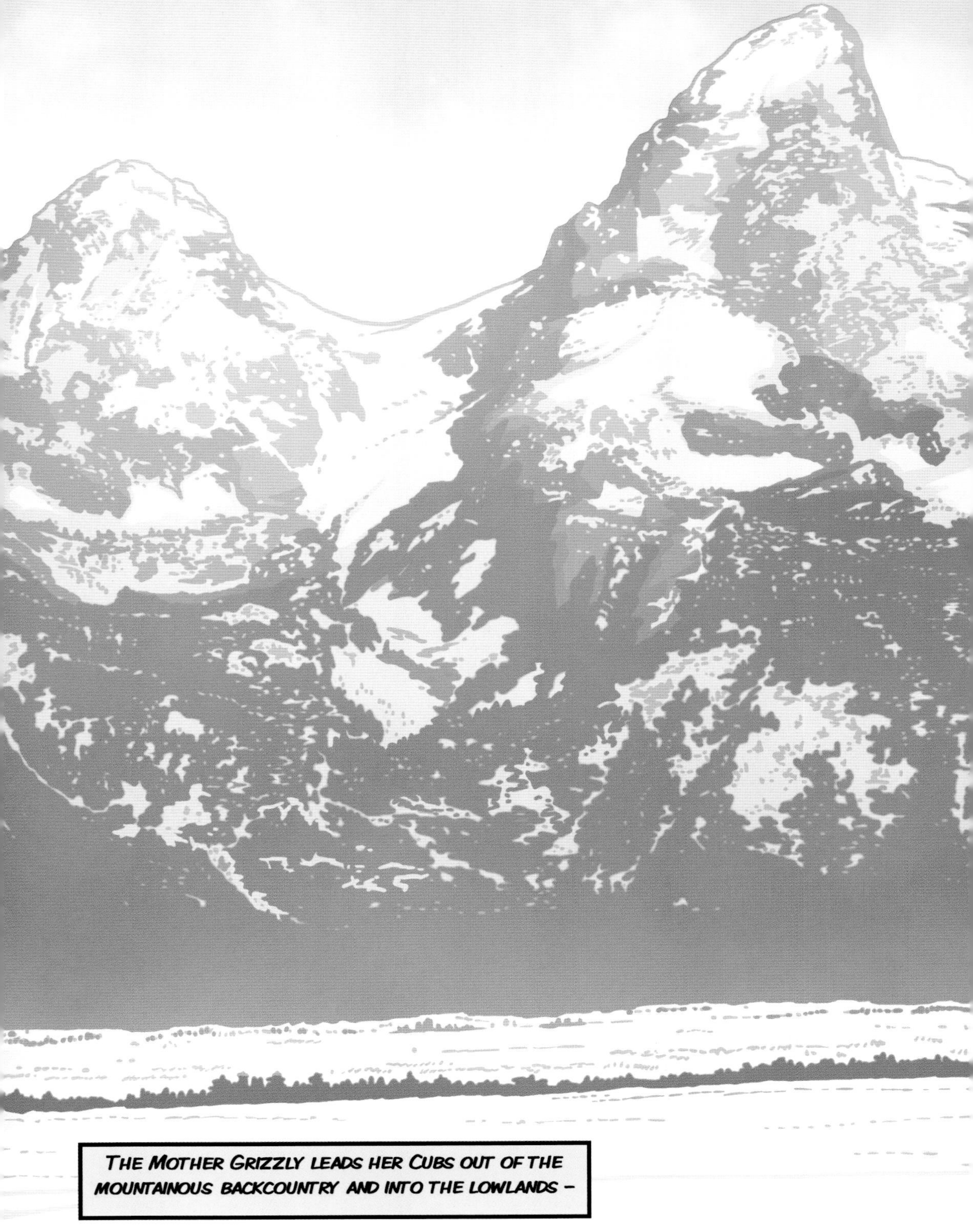
THE MOTHER GRIZZLY LEADS HER CUBS OUT OF THE MOUNTAINOUS BACKCOUNTRY AND INTO THE LOWLANDS –

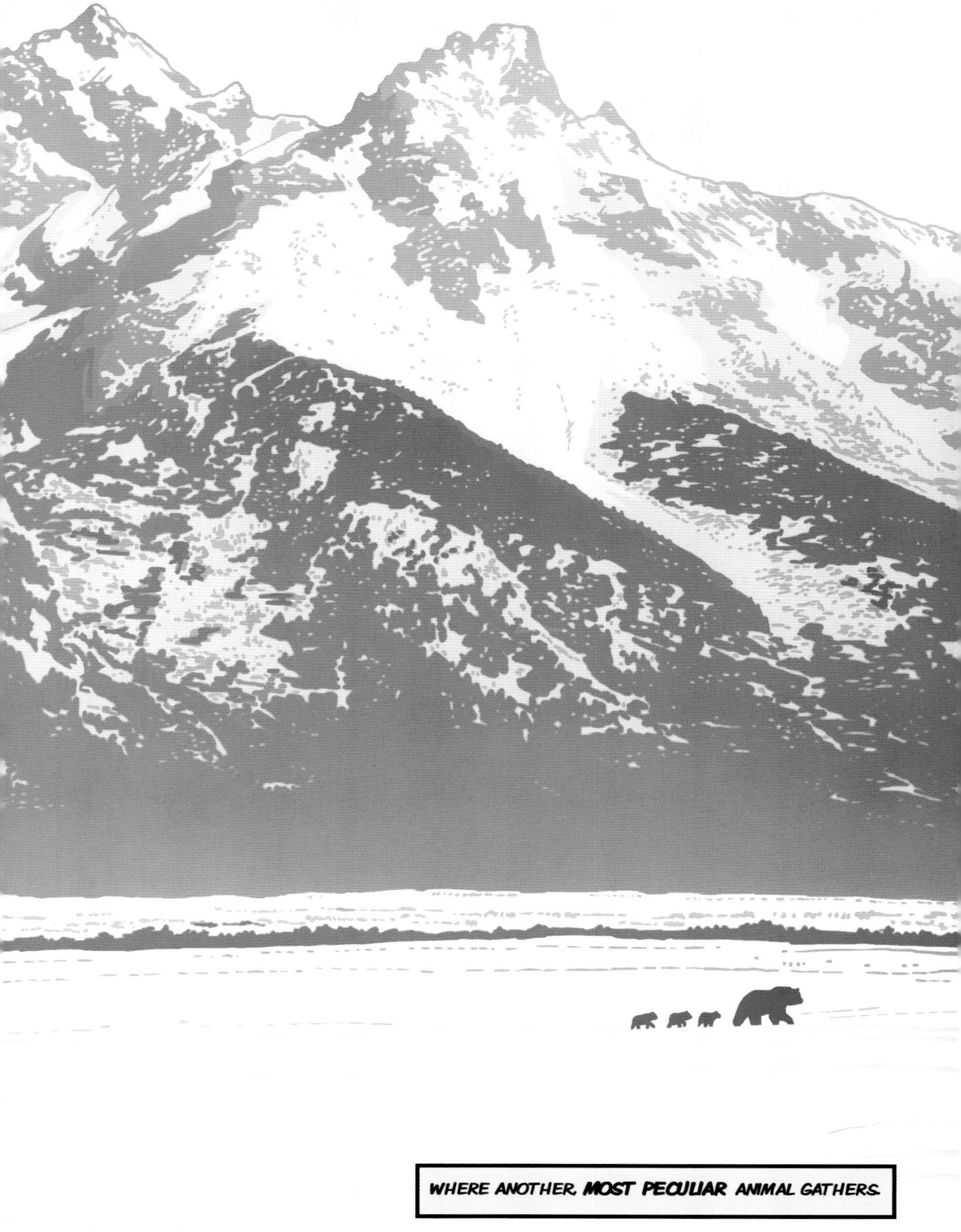
WHERE ANOTHER, MOST PECULIAR ANIMAL GATHERS.

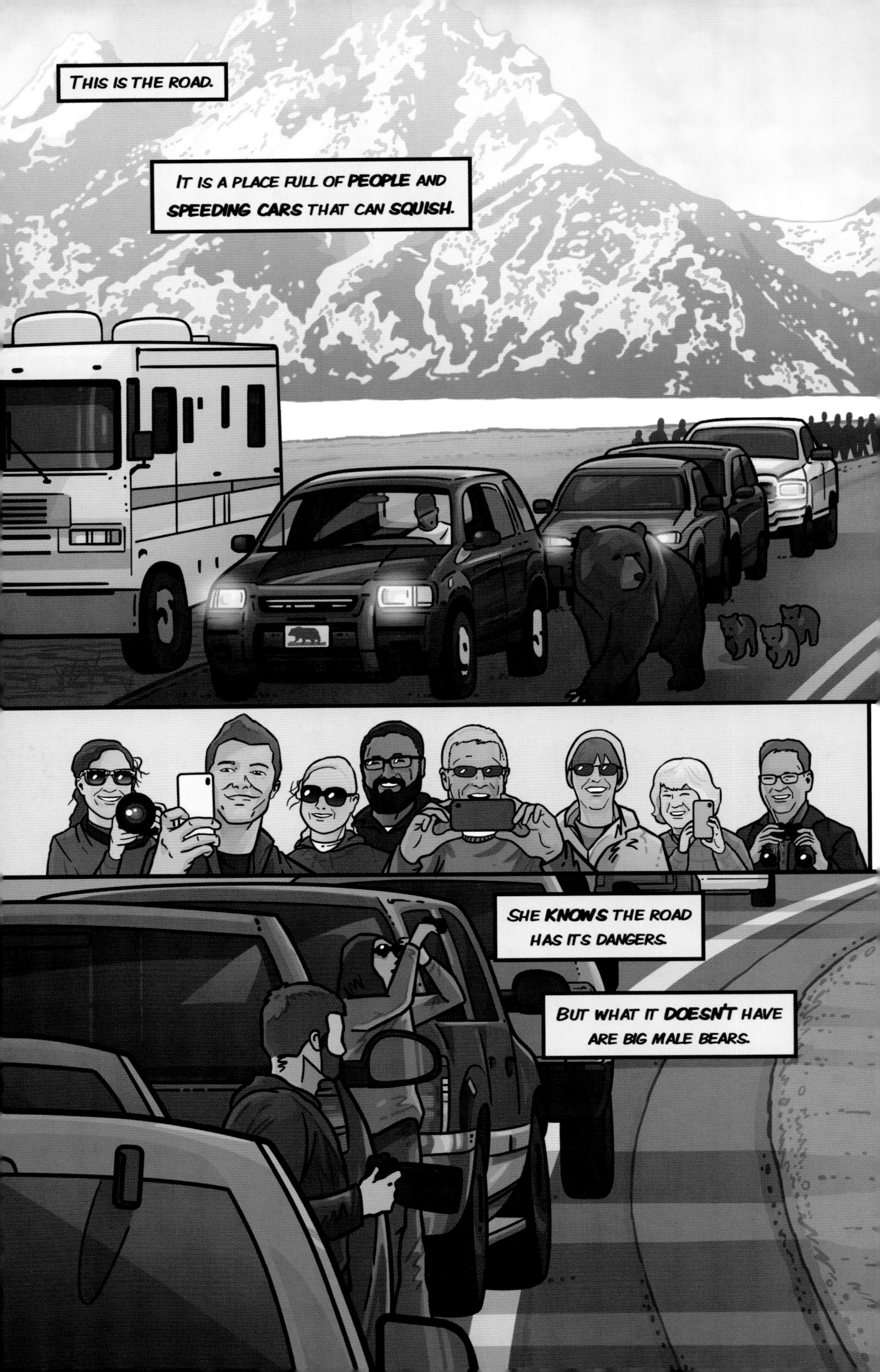
THIS IS THE ROAD.
IT IS A PLACE FULL OF PEOPLE AND SPEEDING CARS THAT CAN SQUISH.
SHE KNOWS THE ROAD HAS ITS DANGERS.
BUT WHAT IT DOESN'T HAVE ARE BIG MALE BEARS.

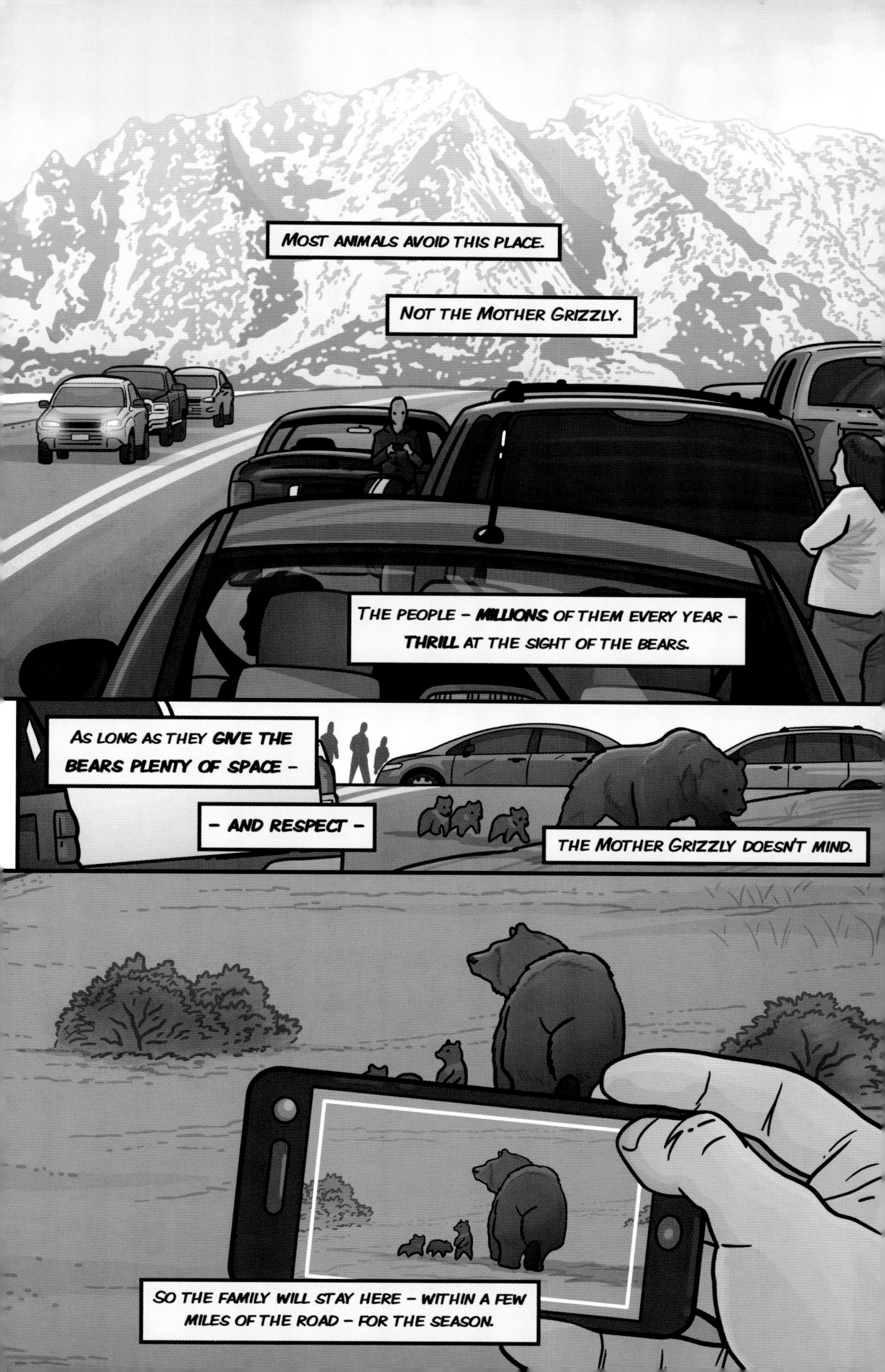
MOST ANIMALS AVOID THIS PLACE.
NOT THE MOTHER GRIZZLY.
THE PEOPLE – MILLIONS OF THEM EVERY YEAR – THRILL AT THE SIGHT OF THE BEARS.
AS LONG AS THEY GIVE THE BEARS PLENTY OF SPACE –
– AND RESPECT –
THE MOTHER GRIZZLY DOESN'T MIND.
SO THE FAMILY WILL STAY HERE – WITHIN A FEW MILES OF THE ROAD – FOR THE SEASON.

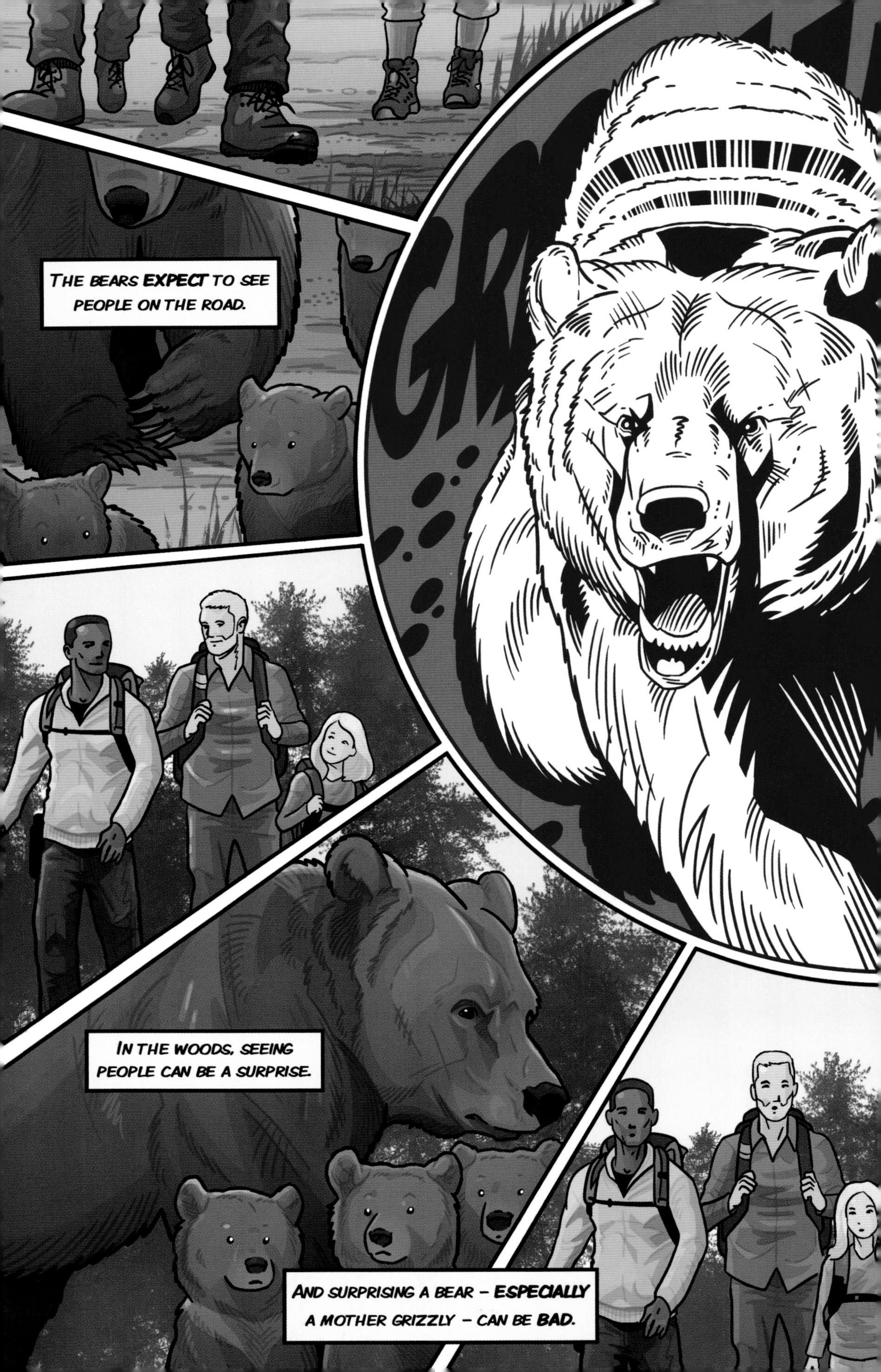
THE BEARS EXPECT TO SEE PEOPLE ON THE ROAD.
IN THE WOODS, SEEING PEOPLE CAN BE A SURPRISE.
AND SURPRISING A BEAR – ESPECIALLY A MOTHER GRIZZLY – CAN BE BAD.

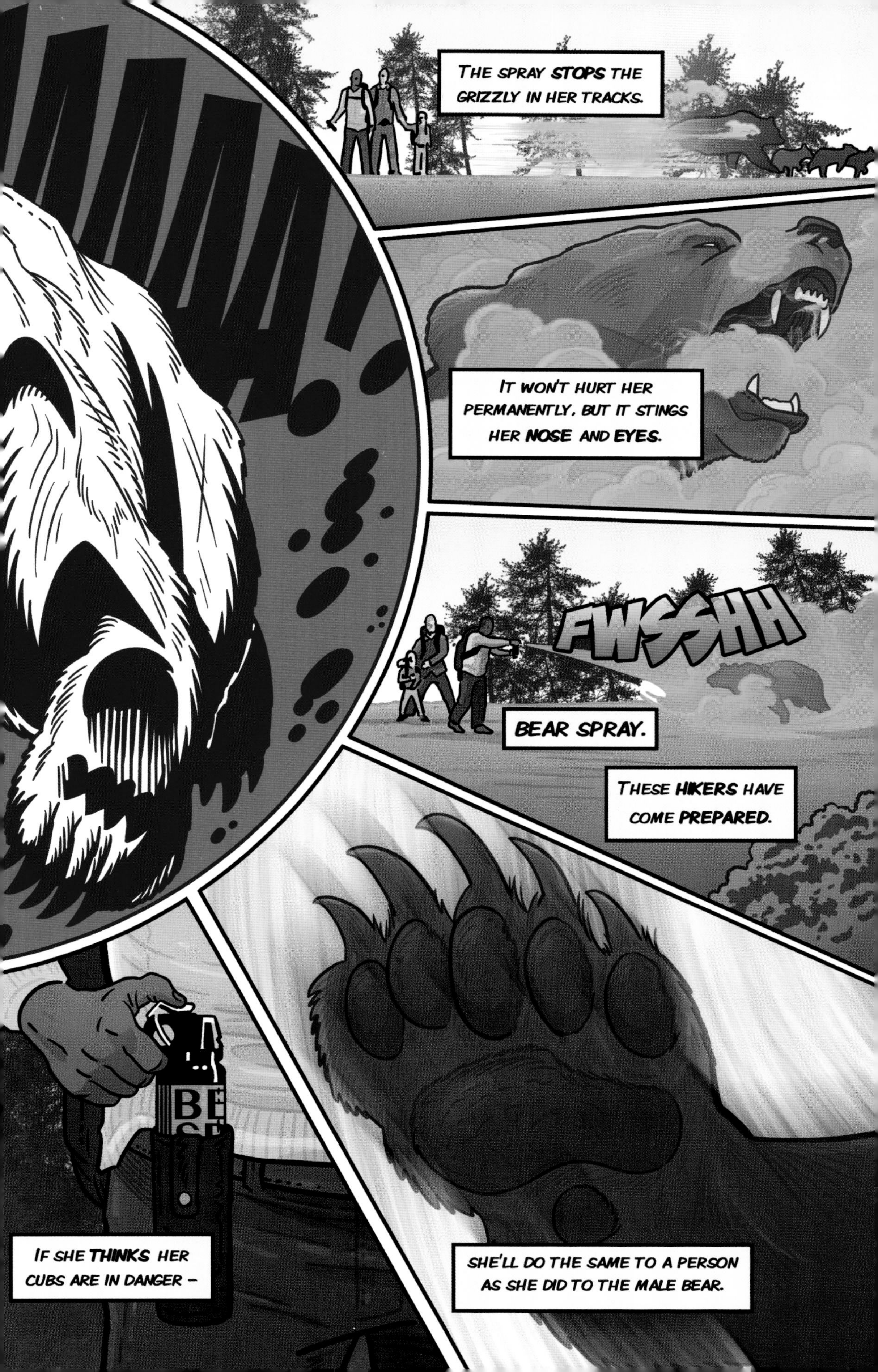
THE SPRAY STOPS THE GRIZZLY IN HER TRACKS.
IT WON'T HURT HER PERMANENTLY, BUT IT STINGS HER NOSE AND EYES.
FWSSHH
BEAR SPRAY.
THESE HIKERS HAVE COME PREPARED.
IF SHE THINKS HER CUBS ARE IN DANGER –
SHE'LL DO THE SAME TO A PERSON AS SHE DID TO THE MALE BEAR.

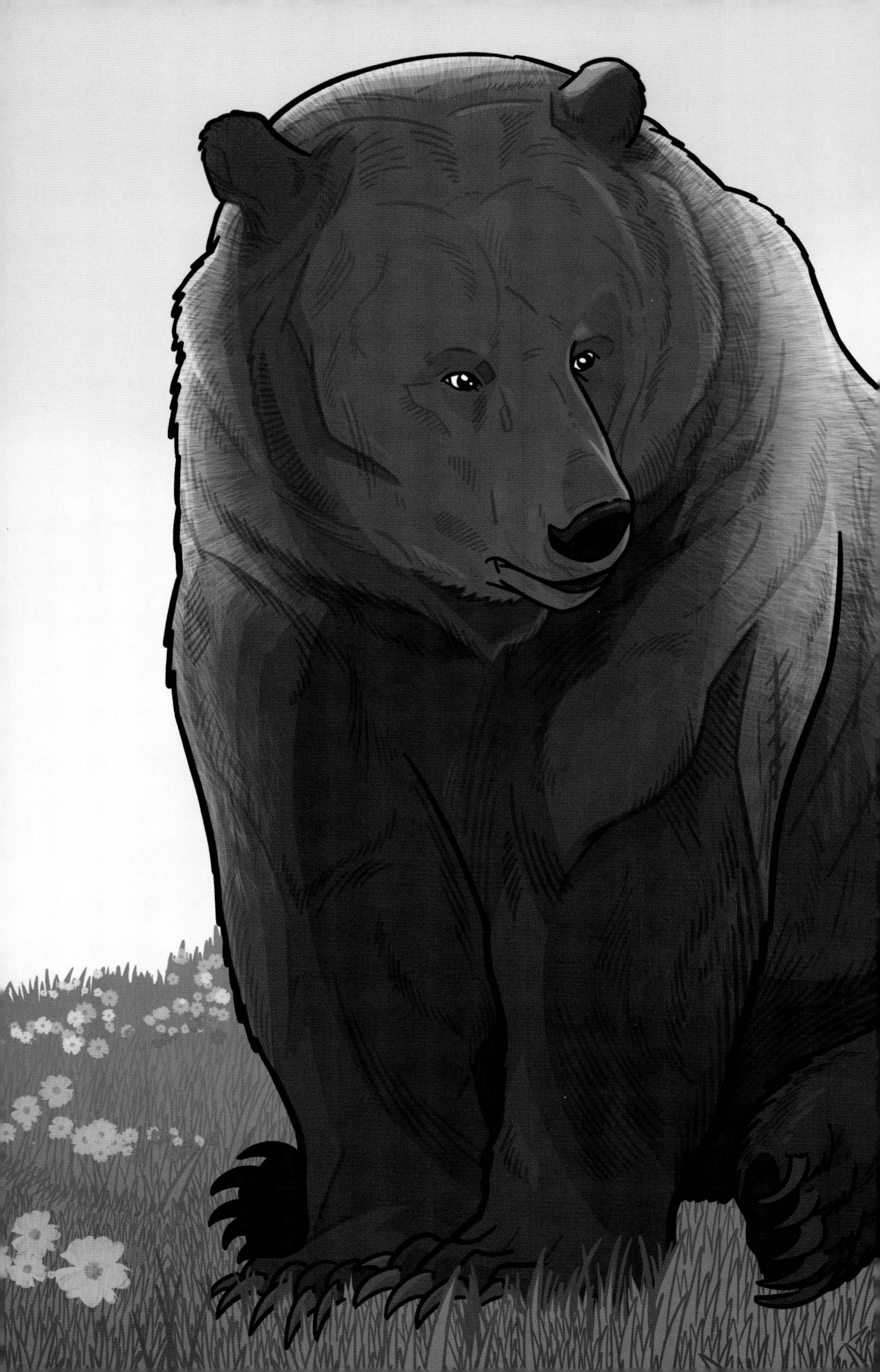

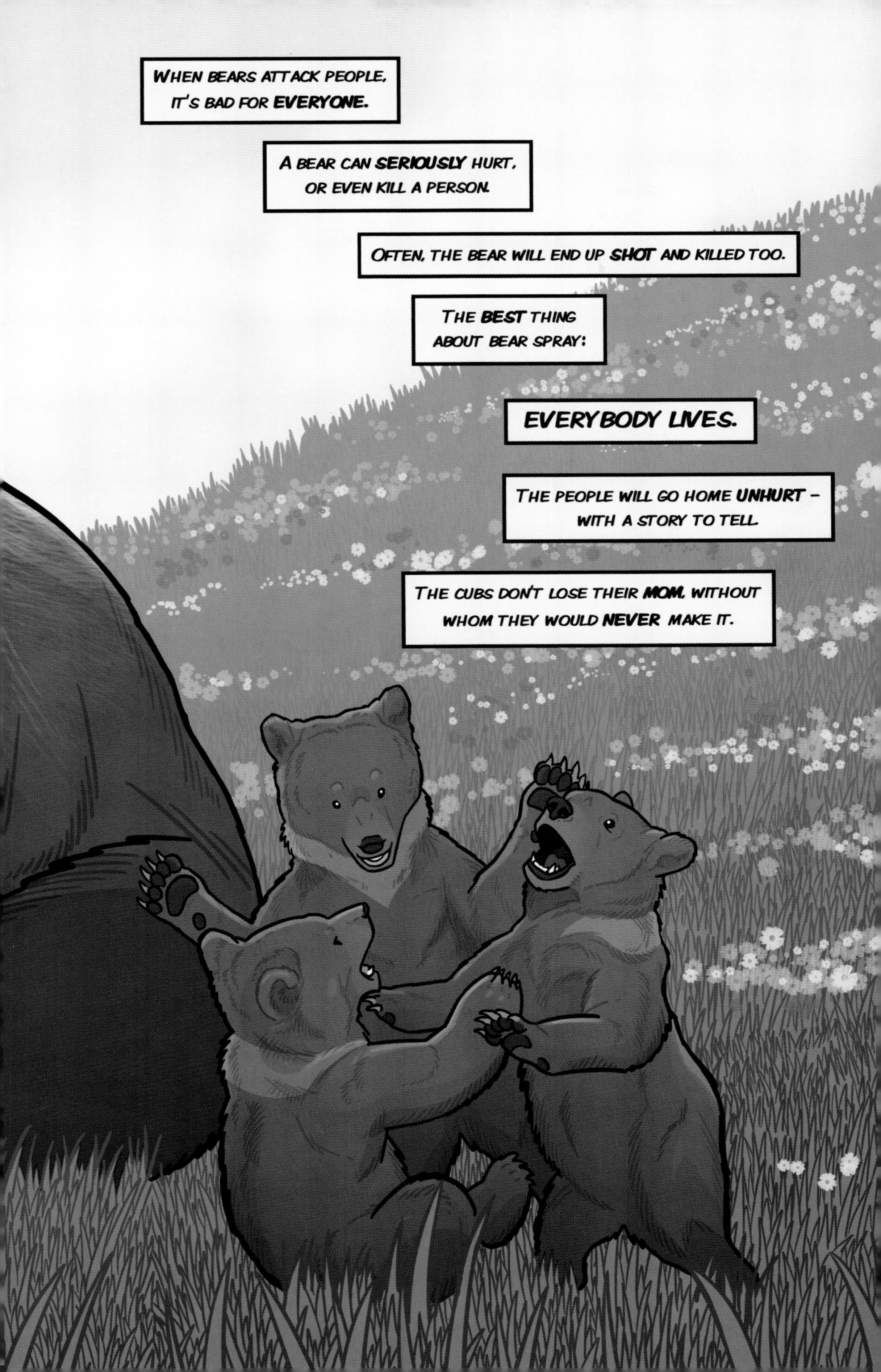
WHEN BEARS ATTACK PEOPLE, IT'S BAD FOR EVERYONE.
A BEAR CAN SERIOUSLY HURT, OR EVEN KILL A PERSON.
OFTEN, THE BEAR WILL END UP SHOT AND KILLED TOO.
THE BEST THING ABOUT BEAR SPRAY:
EVERYBODY LIVES.
THE PEOPLE WILL GO HOME UNHURT – WITH A STORY TO TELL.
THE CUBS DON'T LOSE THEIR MOM, WITHOUT WHOM THEY WOULD NEVER MAKE IT.

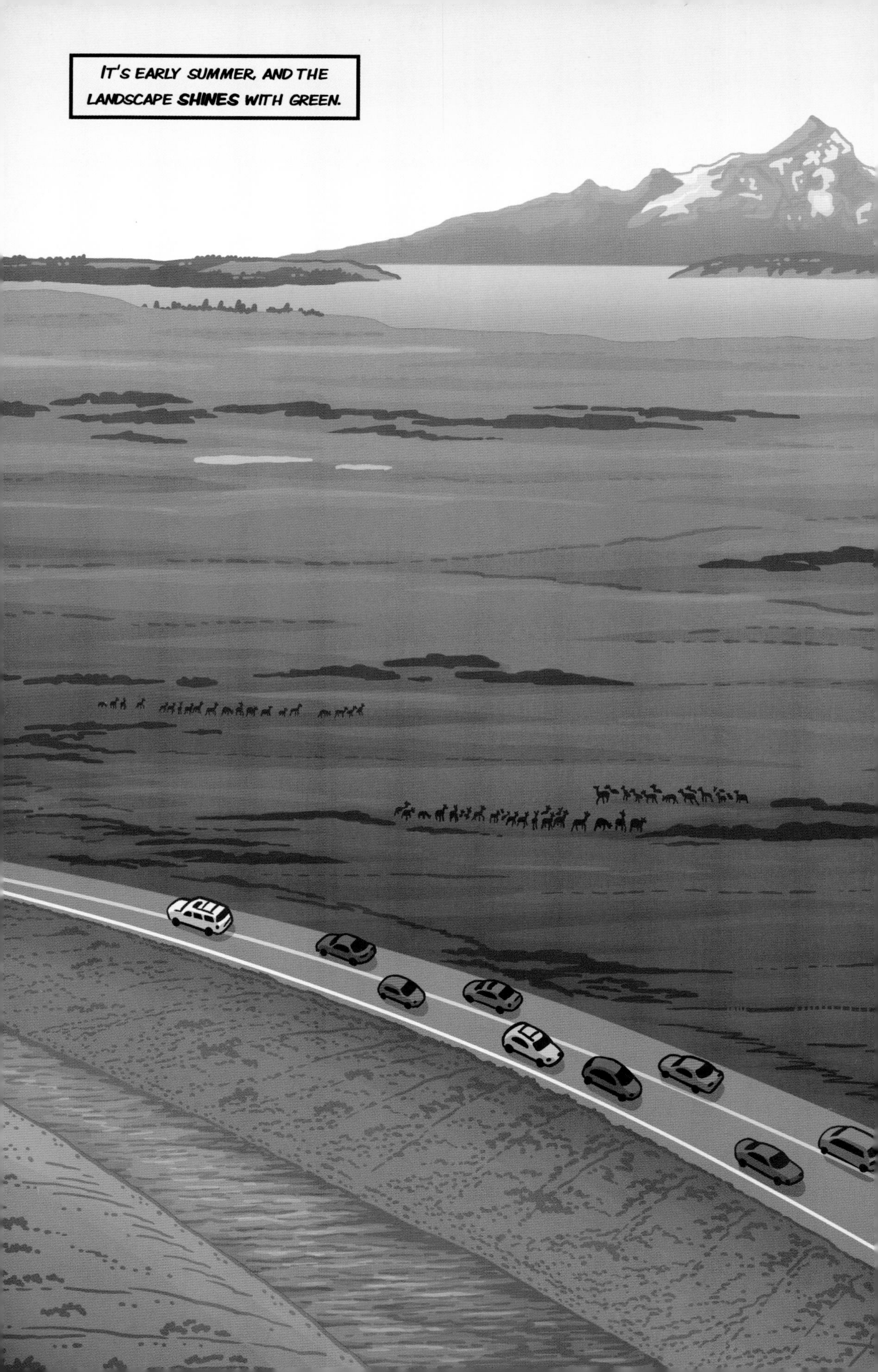
IT'S EARLY SUMMER, AND THE LANDSCAPE SHINES WITH GREEN.

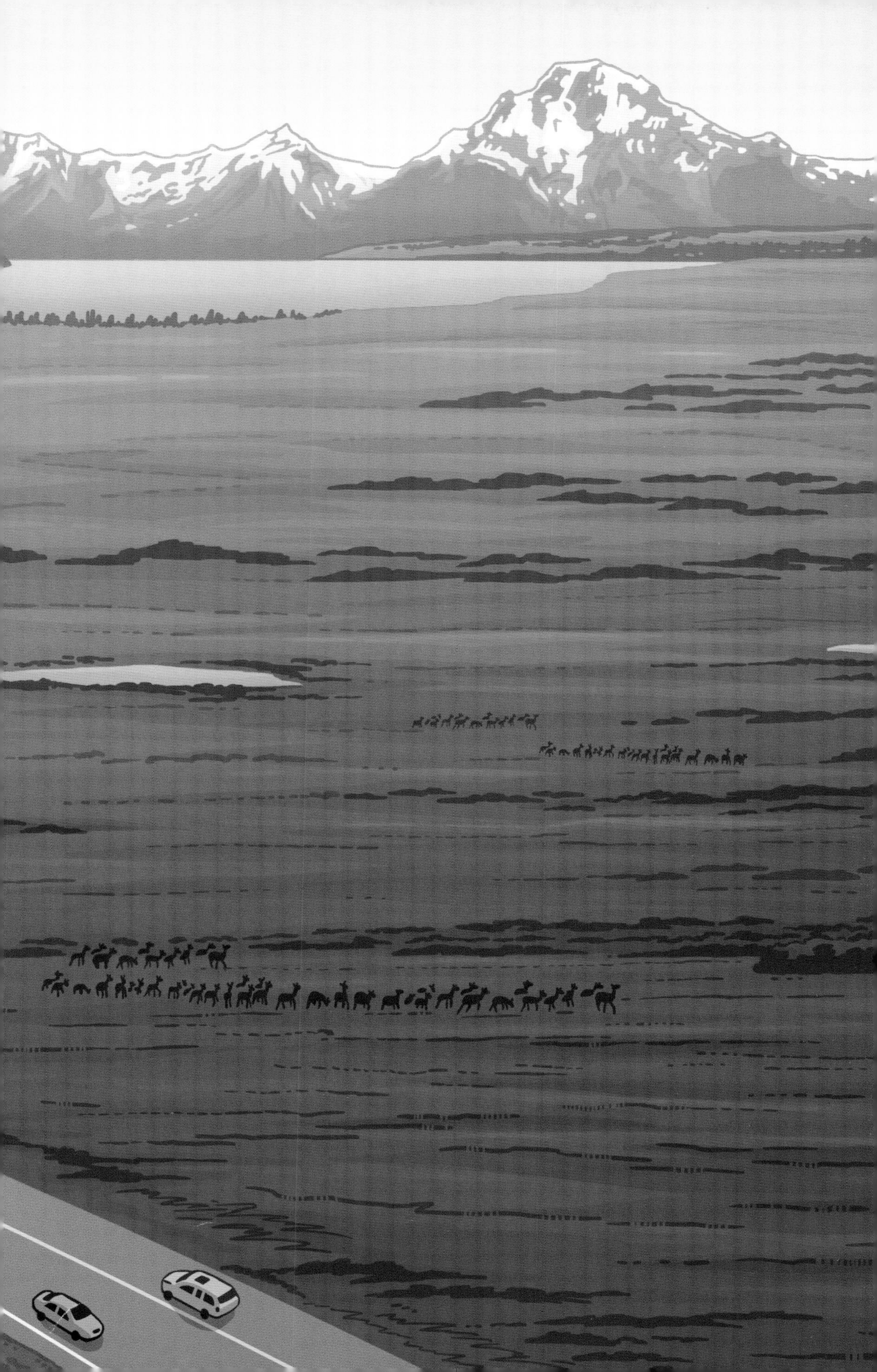

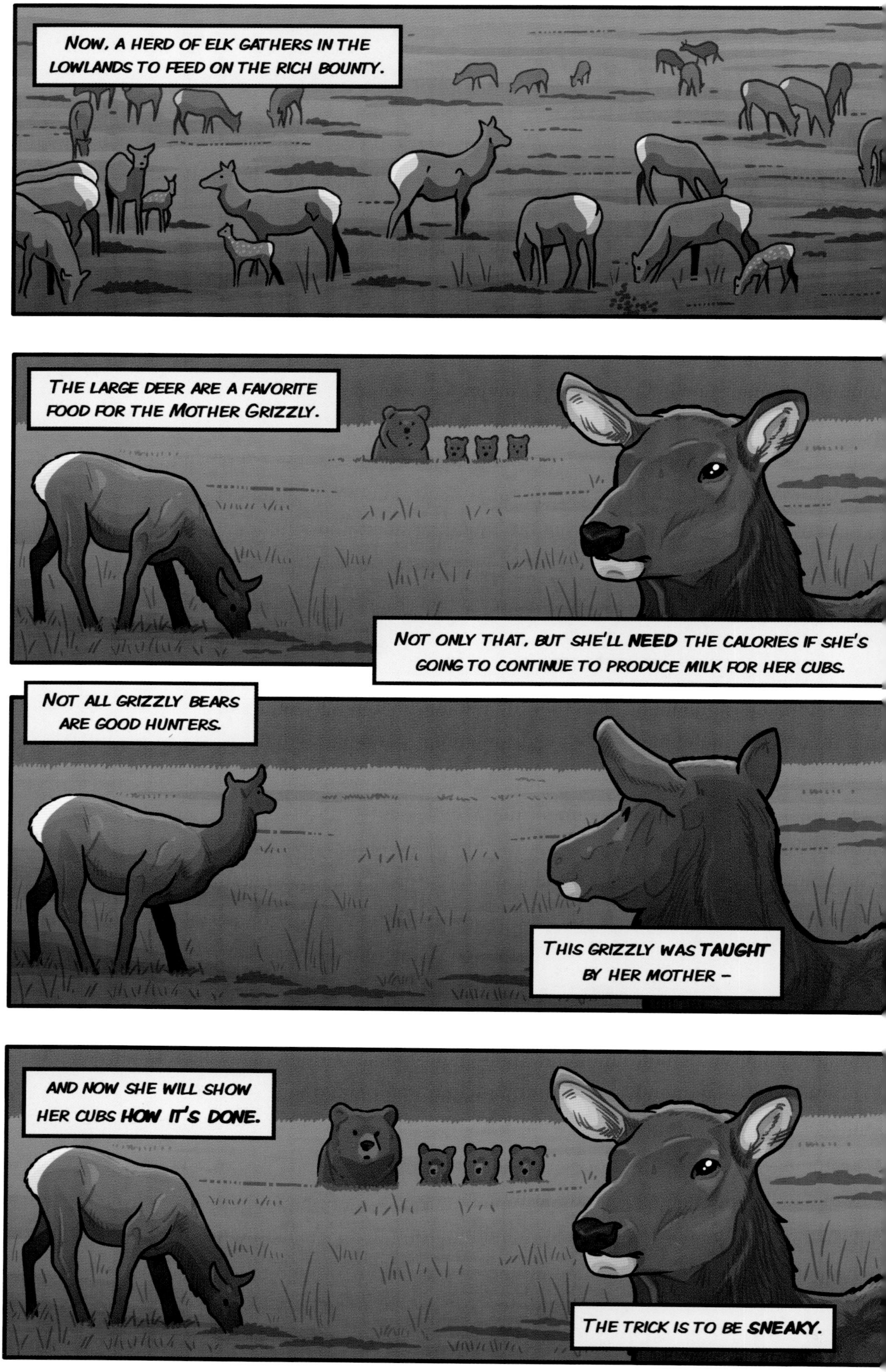
NOW, A HERD OF ELK GATHERS IN THE LOWLANDS TO FEED ON THE RICH BOUNTY.
THE LARGE DEER ARE A FAVORITE FOOD FOR THE MOTHER GRIZZLY.
NOT ONLY THAT, BUT SHE'LL NEED THE CALORIES IF SHE'S GOING TO CONTINUE TO PRODUCE MILK FOR HER CUBS.
NOT ALL GRIZZLY BEARS ARE GOOD HUNTERS.
THIS GRIZZLY WAS TAUGHT BY HER MOTHER –
AND NOW SHE WILL SHOW HER CUBS HOW IT'S DONE.
THE TRICK IS TO BE SNEAKY.

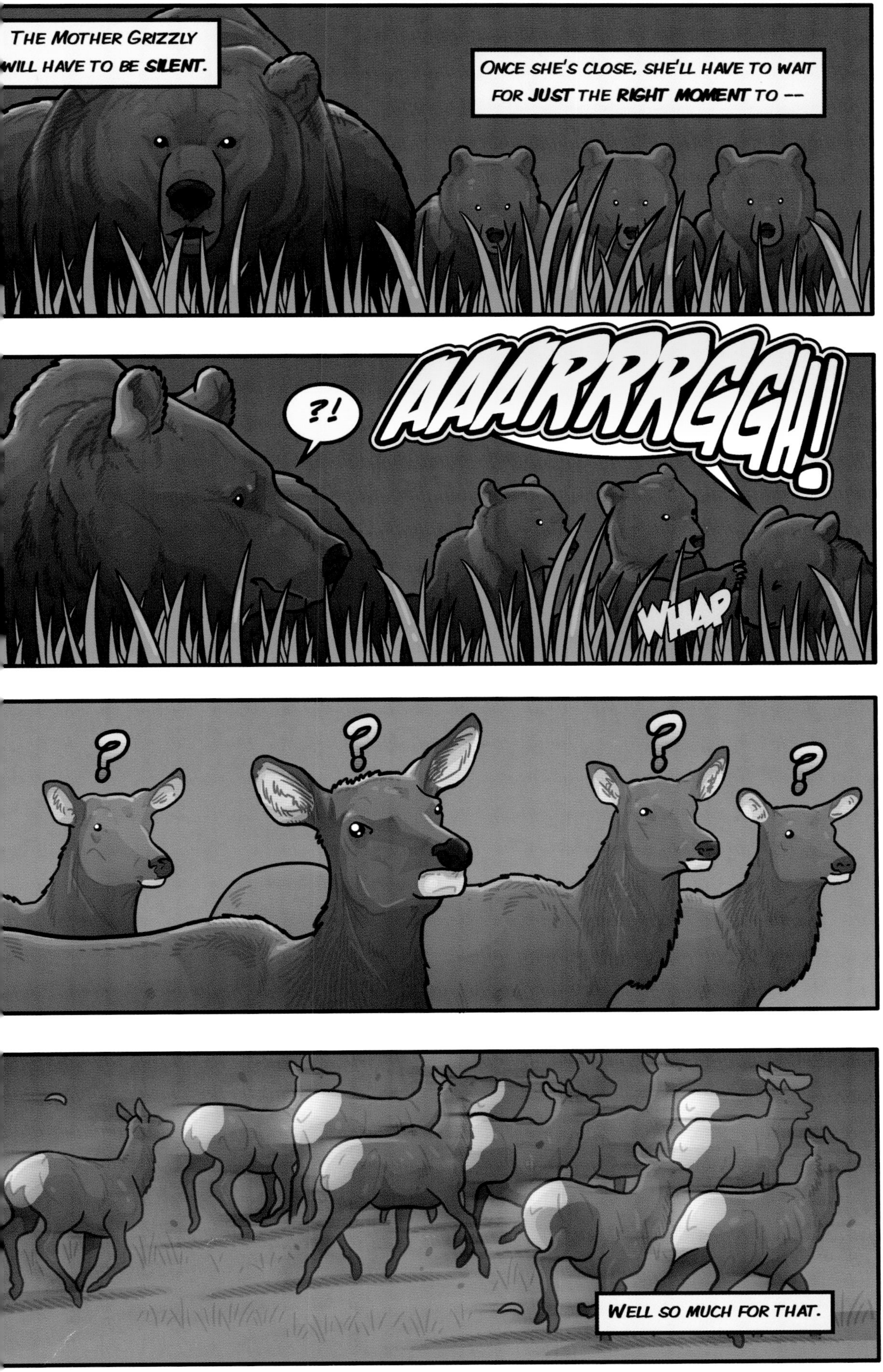
THE MOTHER GRIZZLY WILL HAVE TO BE SILENT.
ONCE SHE'S CLOSE, SHE'LL HAVE TO WAIT FOR JUST THE RIGHT MOMENT TO --
?!
AAAARRRRGGH!
WHAP
?
?
?
?
WELL SO MUCH FOR THAT.

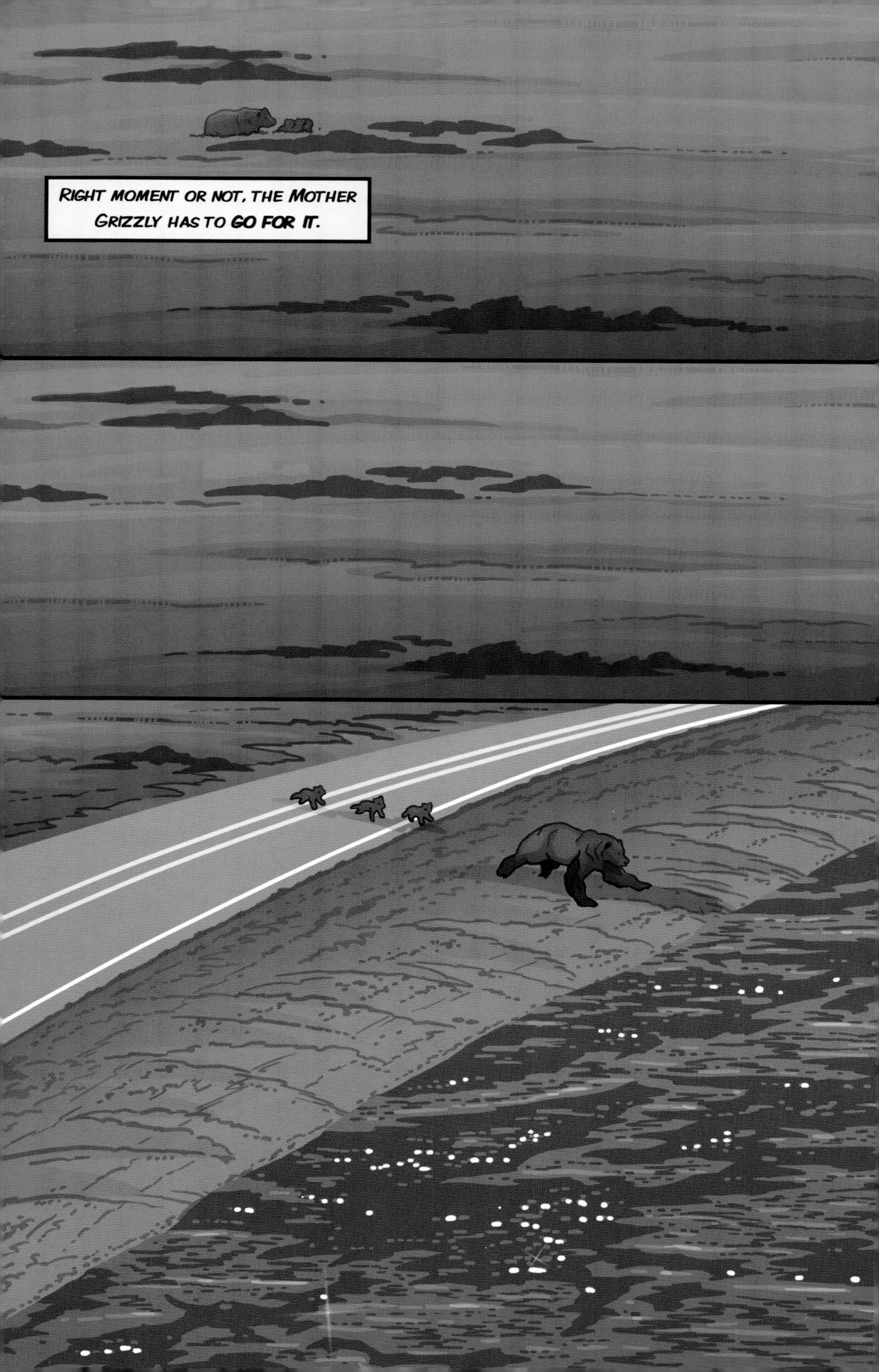
RIGHT MOMENT OR NOT, THE MOTHER GRIZZLY HAS TO GO FOR IT.

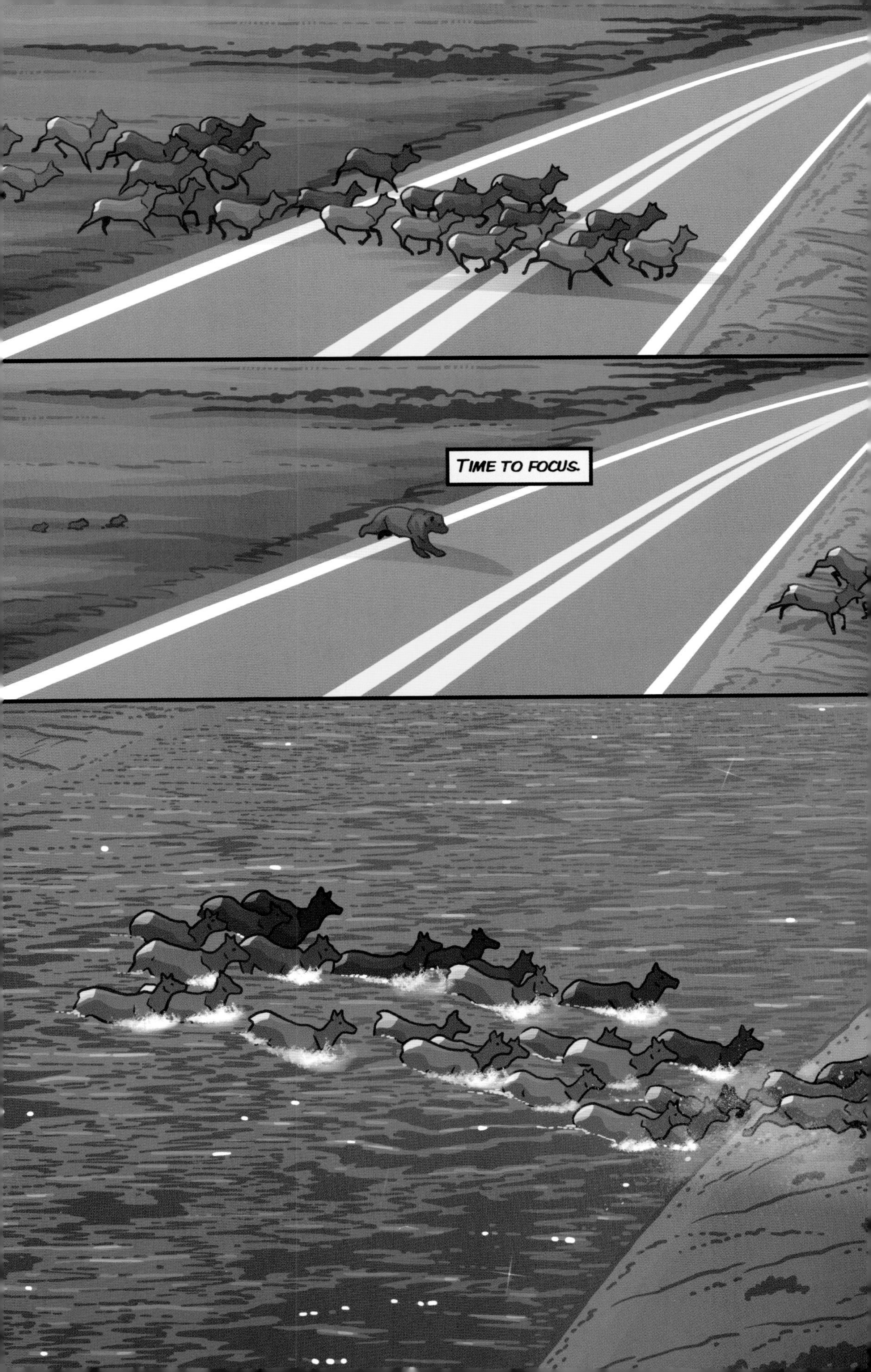
TIME TO FOCUS.

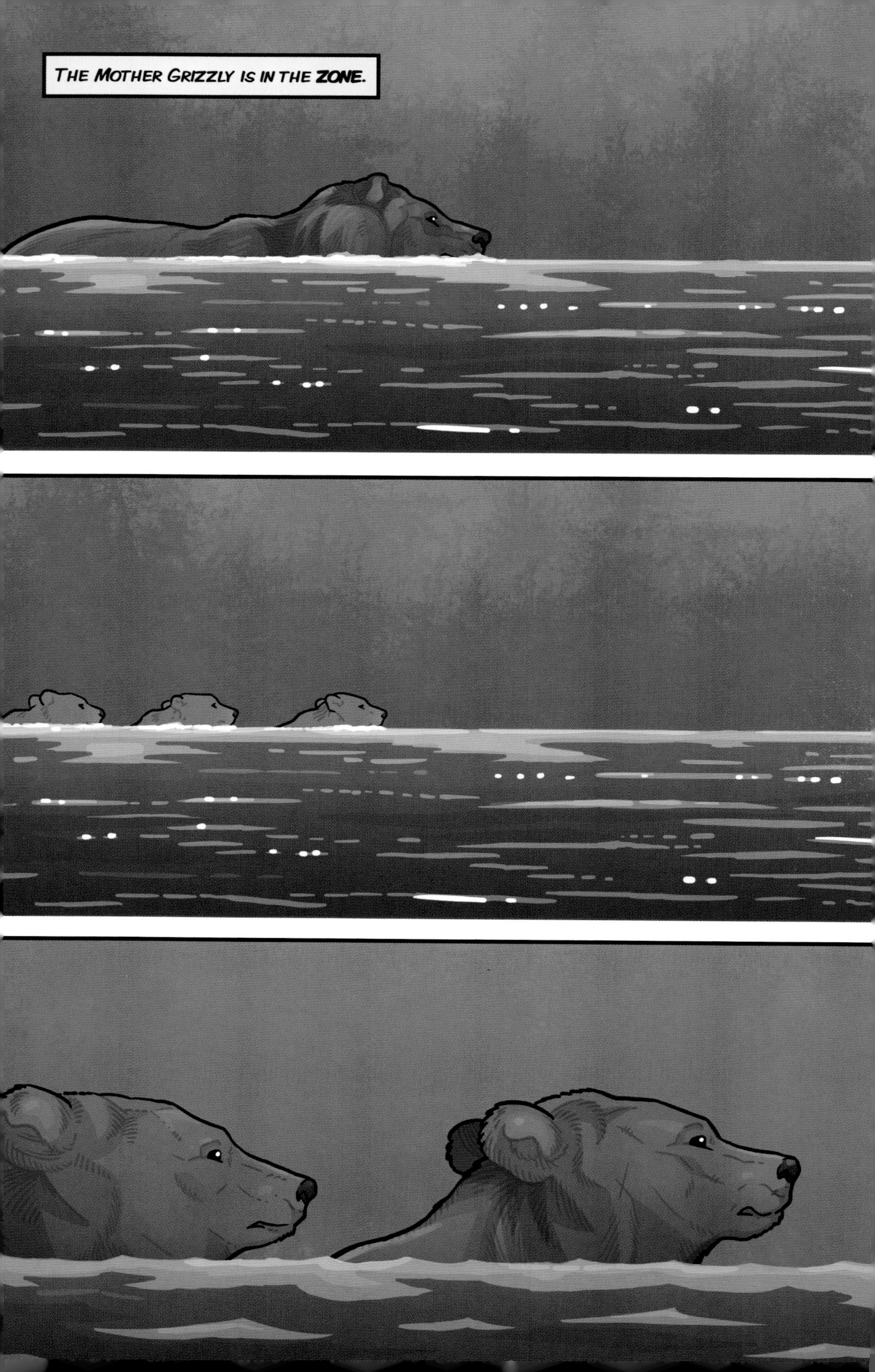
THE MOTHER GRIZZLY IS IN THE ZONE.

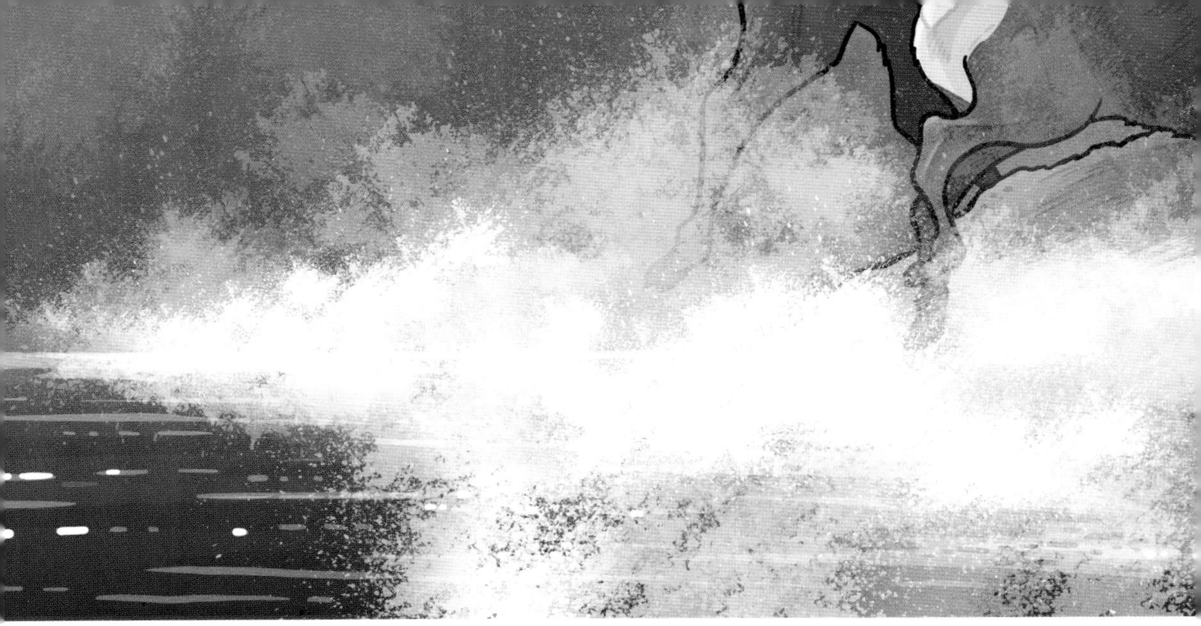

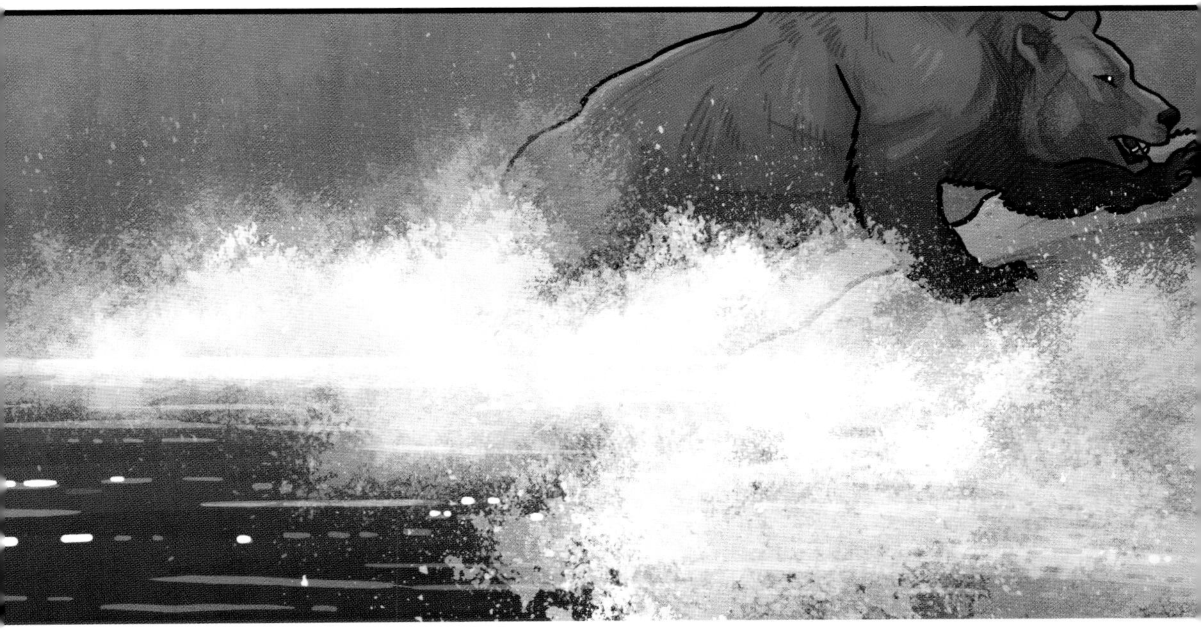

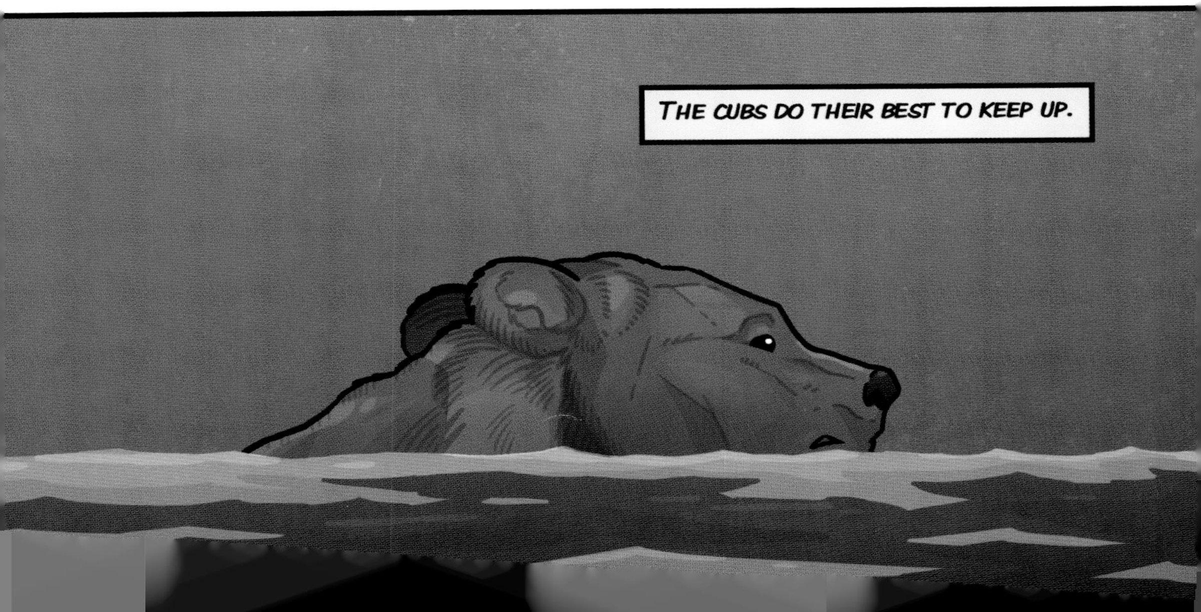
THE CUBS DO THEIR BEST TO KEEP UP.

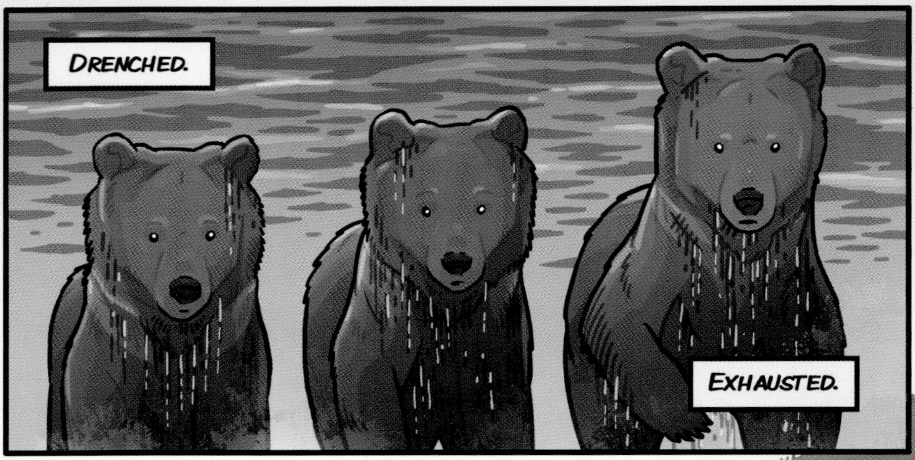
DRENCHED.
EXHAUSTED.
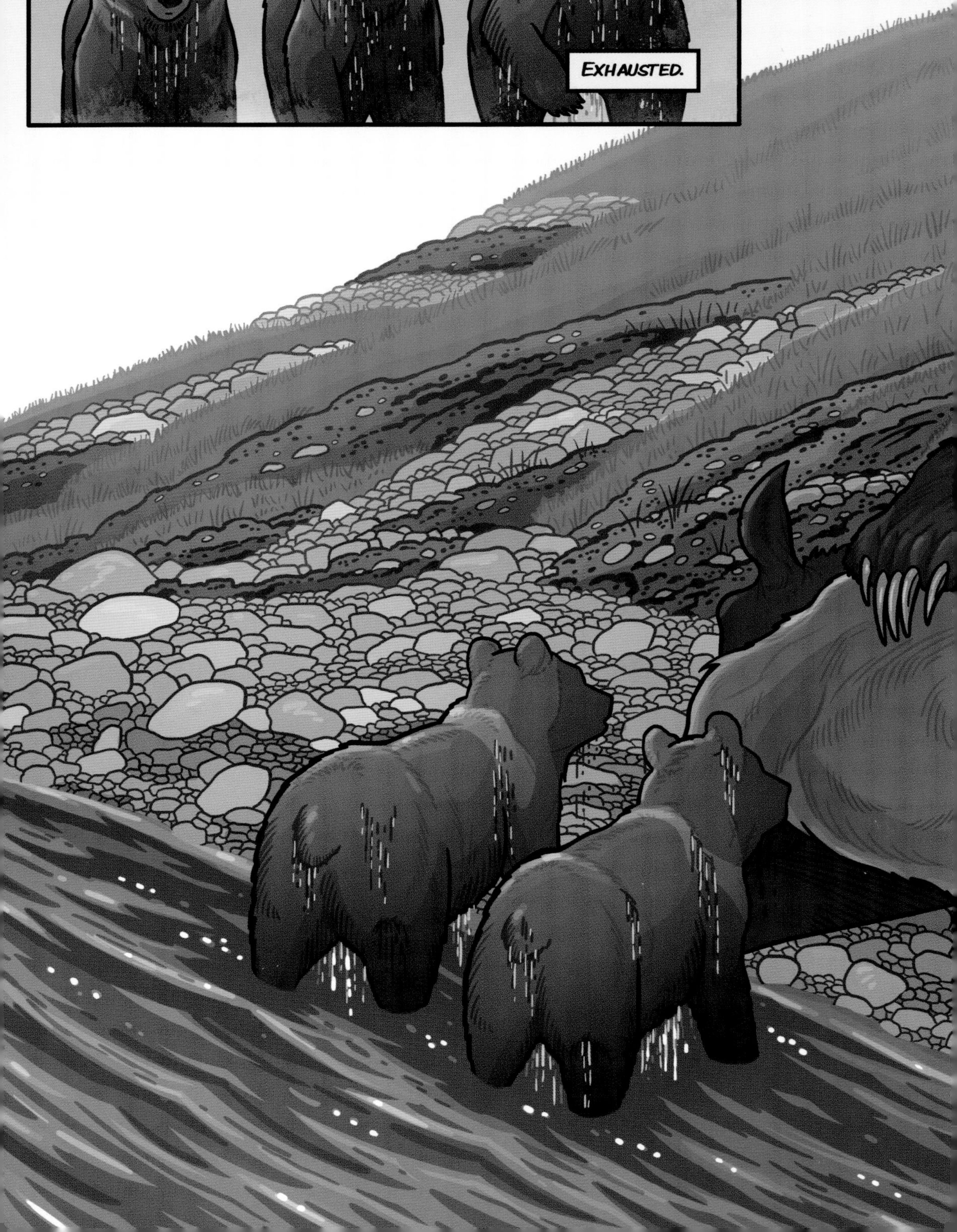

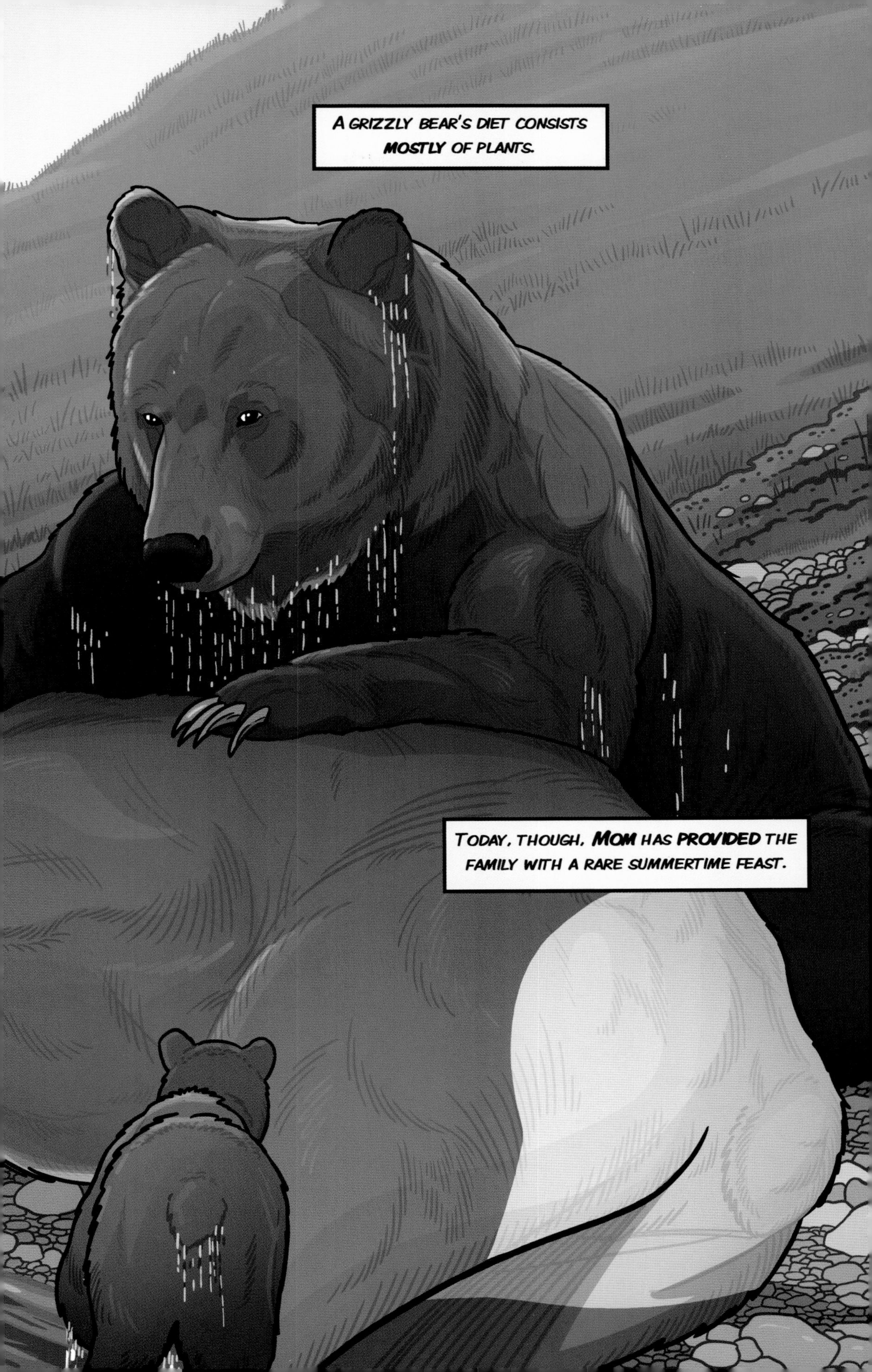
A GRIZZLY BEAR'S DIET CONSISTS MOSTLY OF PLANTS.
TODAY, THOUGH, MOM HAS PROVIDED THE FAMILY WITH A RARE SUMMERTIME FEAST.

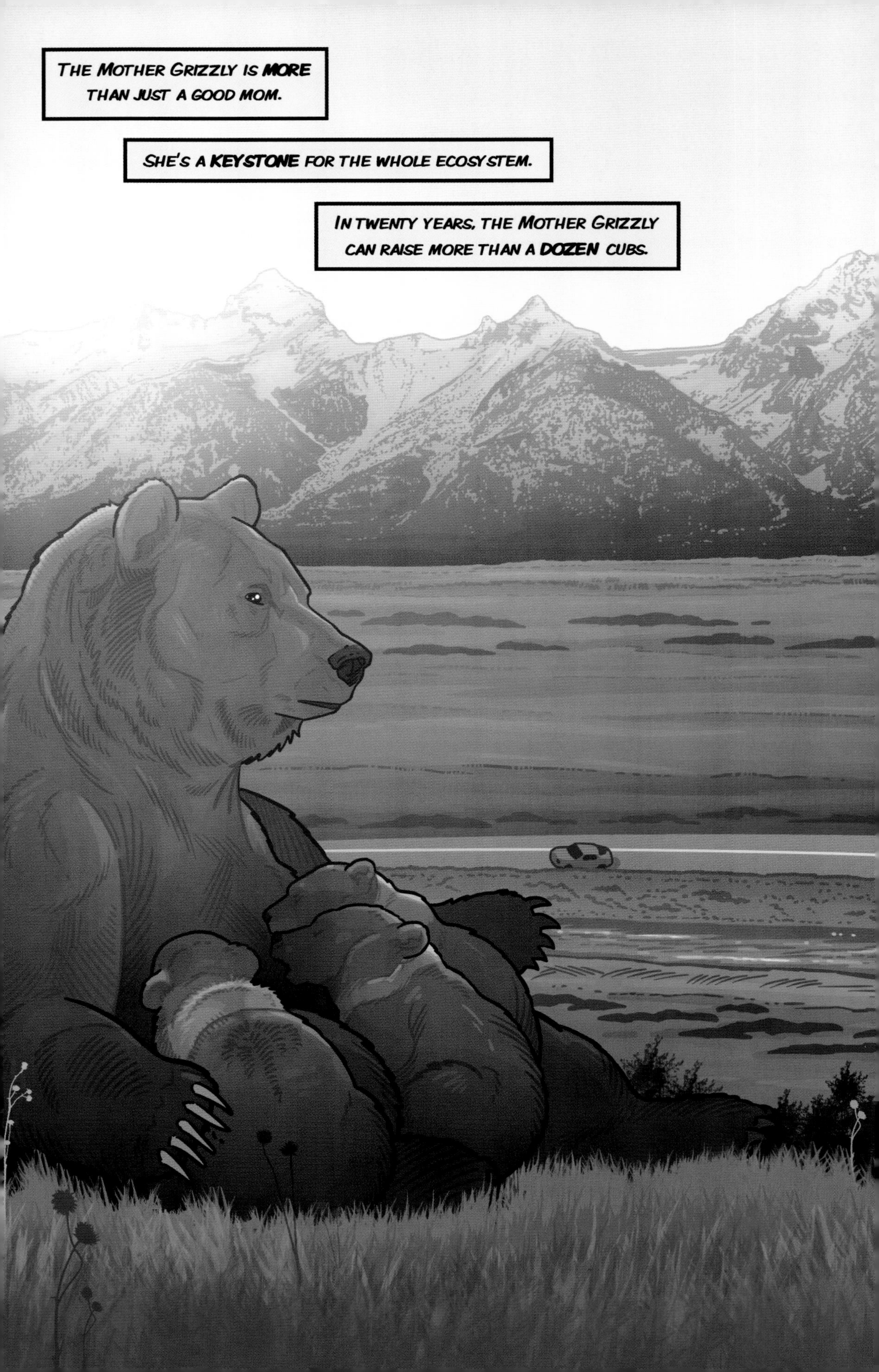
THE MOTHER GRIZZLY IS MORE THAN JUST A GOOD MOM.
SHE'S A KEYSTONE FOR THE WHOLE ECOSYSTEM.
IN TWENTY YEARS, THE MOTHER GRIZZLY CAN RAISE MORE THAN A DOZEN CUBS.

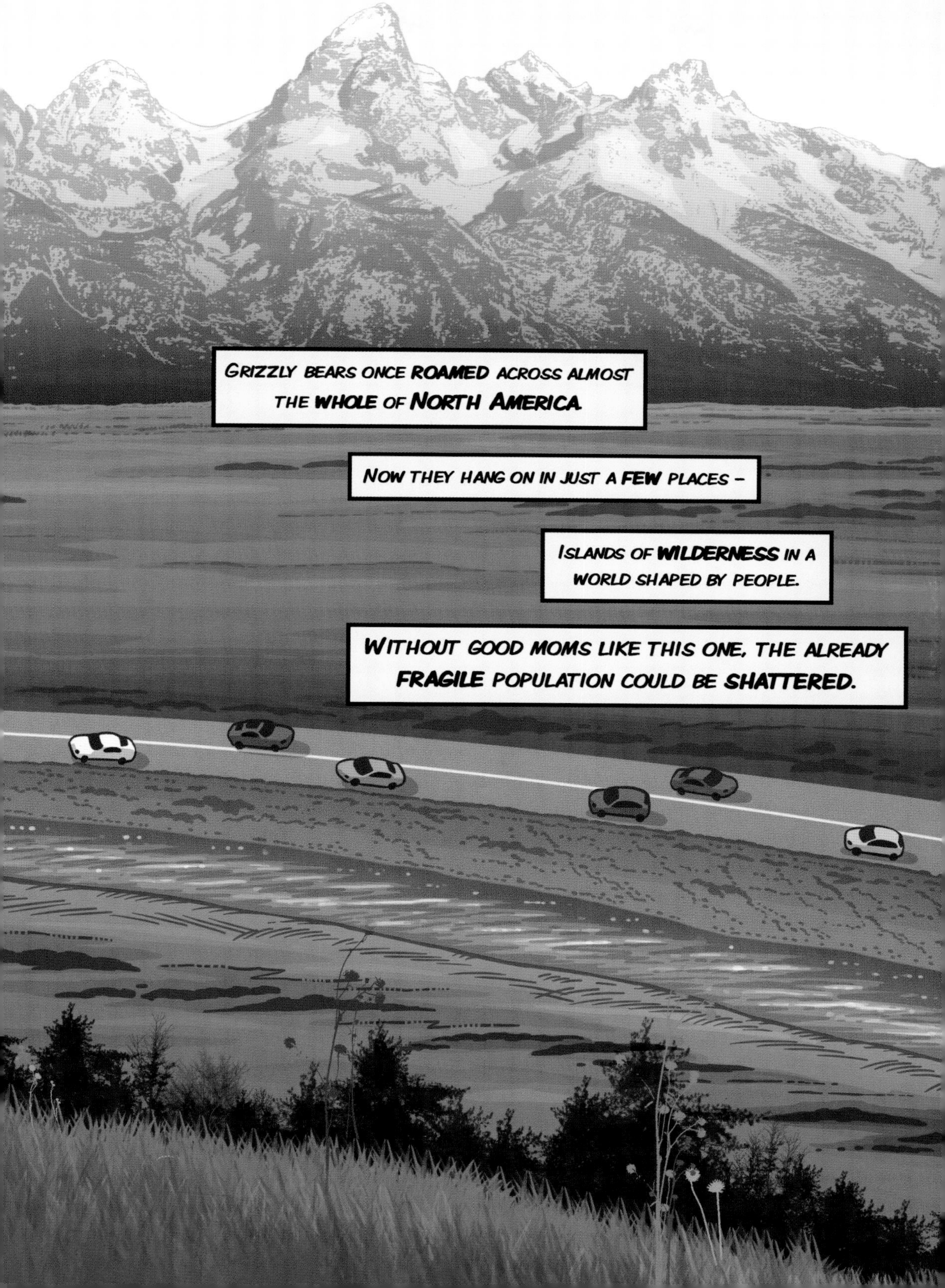
GRIZZLY BEARS ONCE ROAMED ACROSS ALMOST THE WHOLE OF NORTH AMERICA.
NOW THEY HANG ON IN JUST A FEW PLACES –
ISLANDS OF WILDERNESS IN A WORLD SHAPED BY PEOPLE.
WITHOUT GOOD MOMS LIKE THIS ONE, THE ALREADY FRAGILE POPULATION COULD BE SHATTERED.

AMERICAN BLACK BEAR

URSUS AMERICANUS

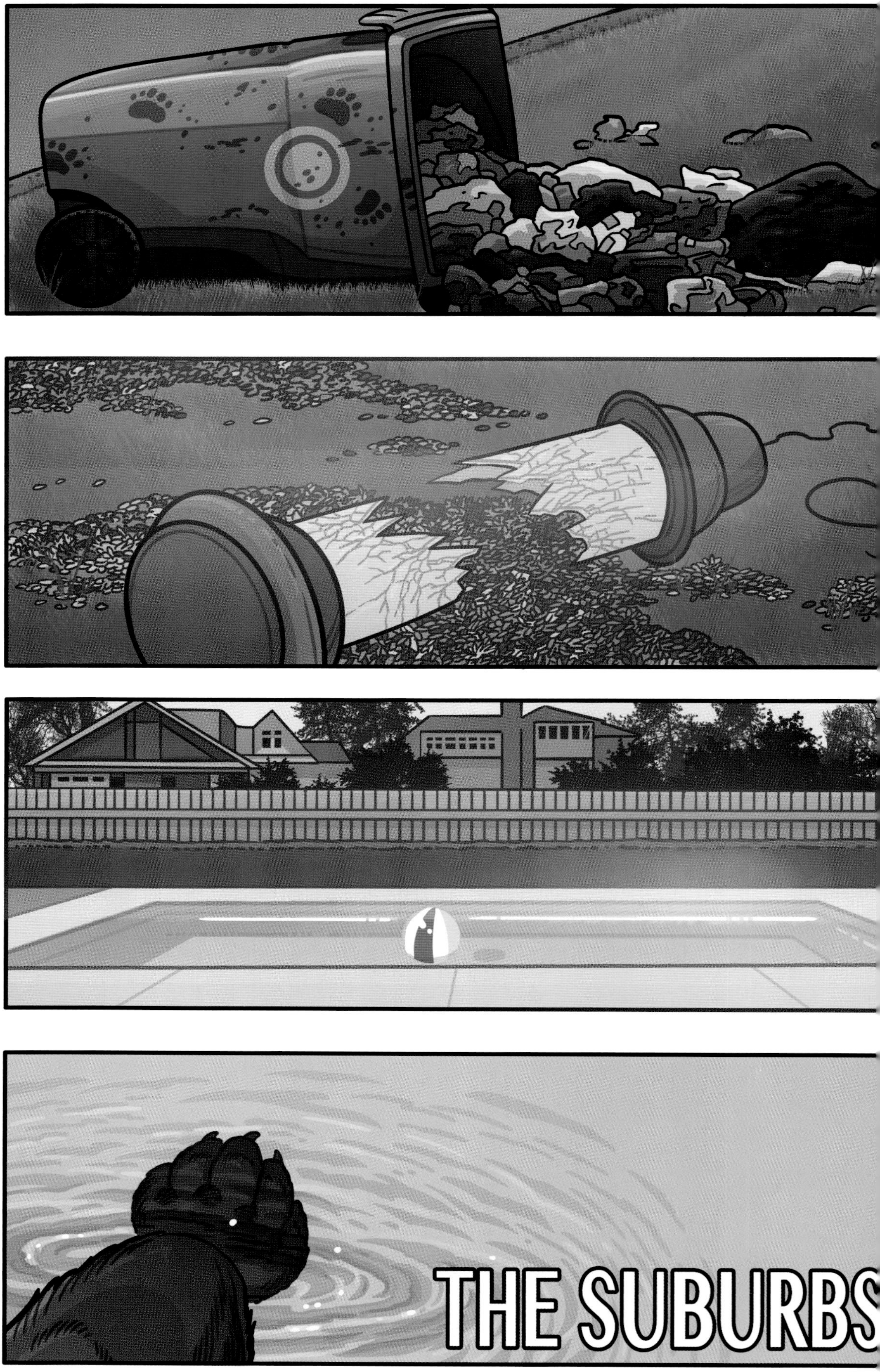
THE SUBURBS

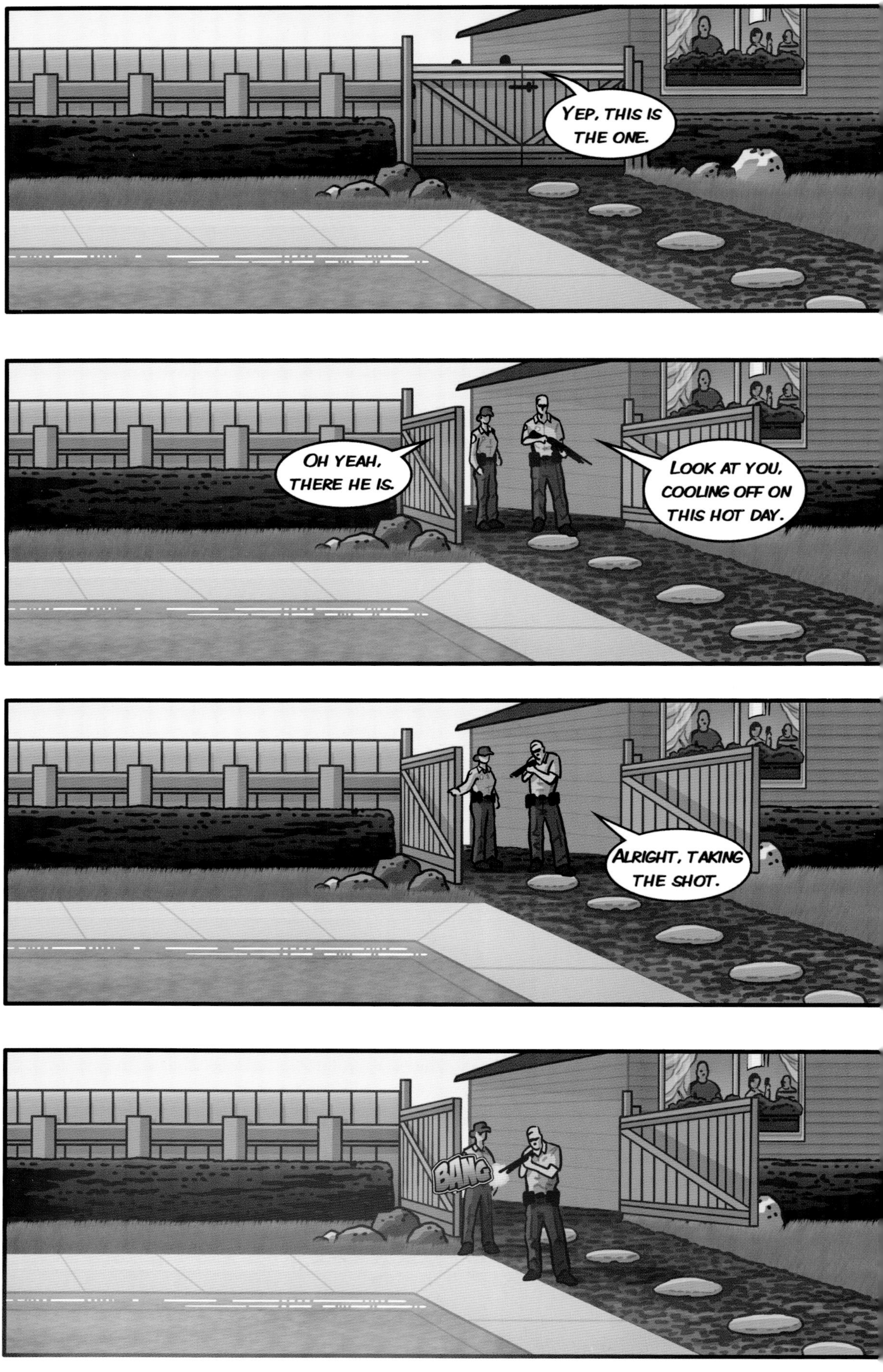
YEP, THIS IS THE ONE.
OH YEAH, THERE HE IS.
LOOK AT YOU, COOLING OFF ON THIS HOT DAY.
ALRIGHT, TAKING THE SHOT.
BANG

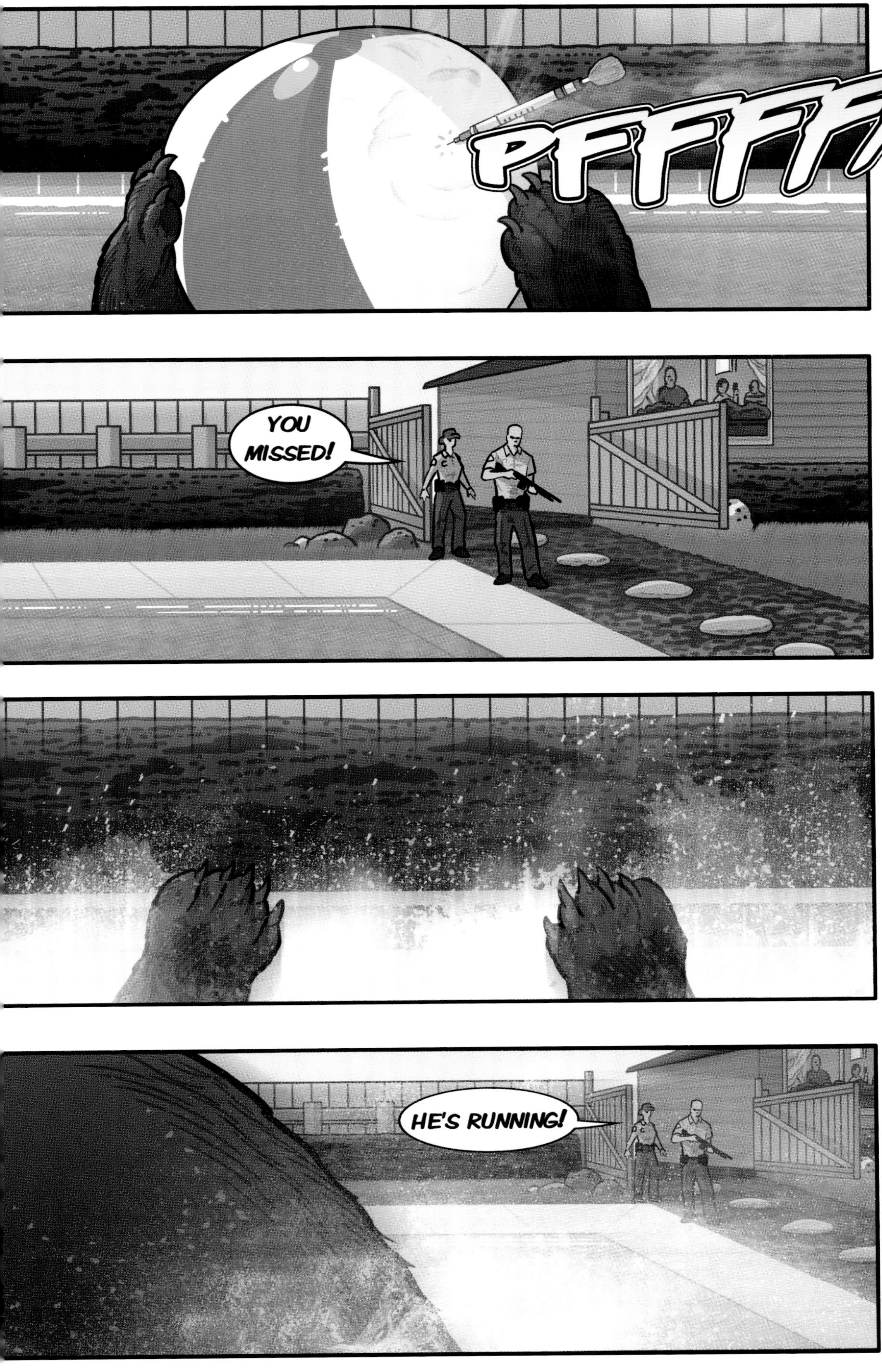
PFFFFT
YOU MISSED!
HE'S RUNNING!

HE'S GOING OVER THE FENCE!
ARF
ARF
WOOF!
LET'S GO!

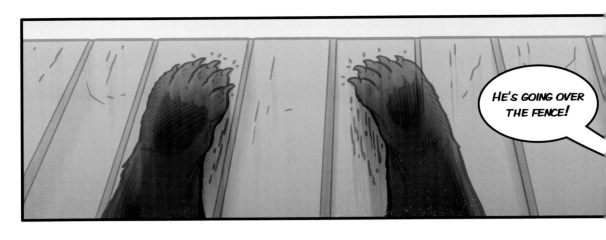

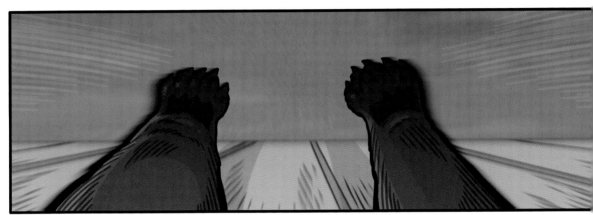

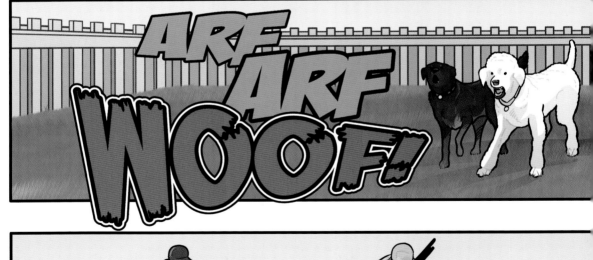

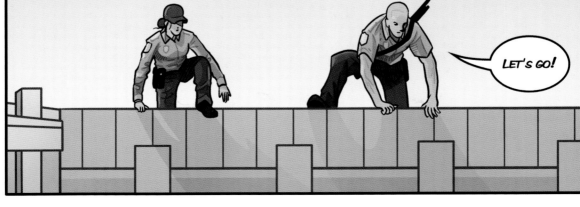

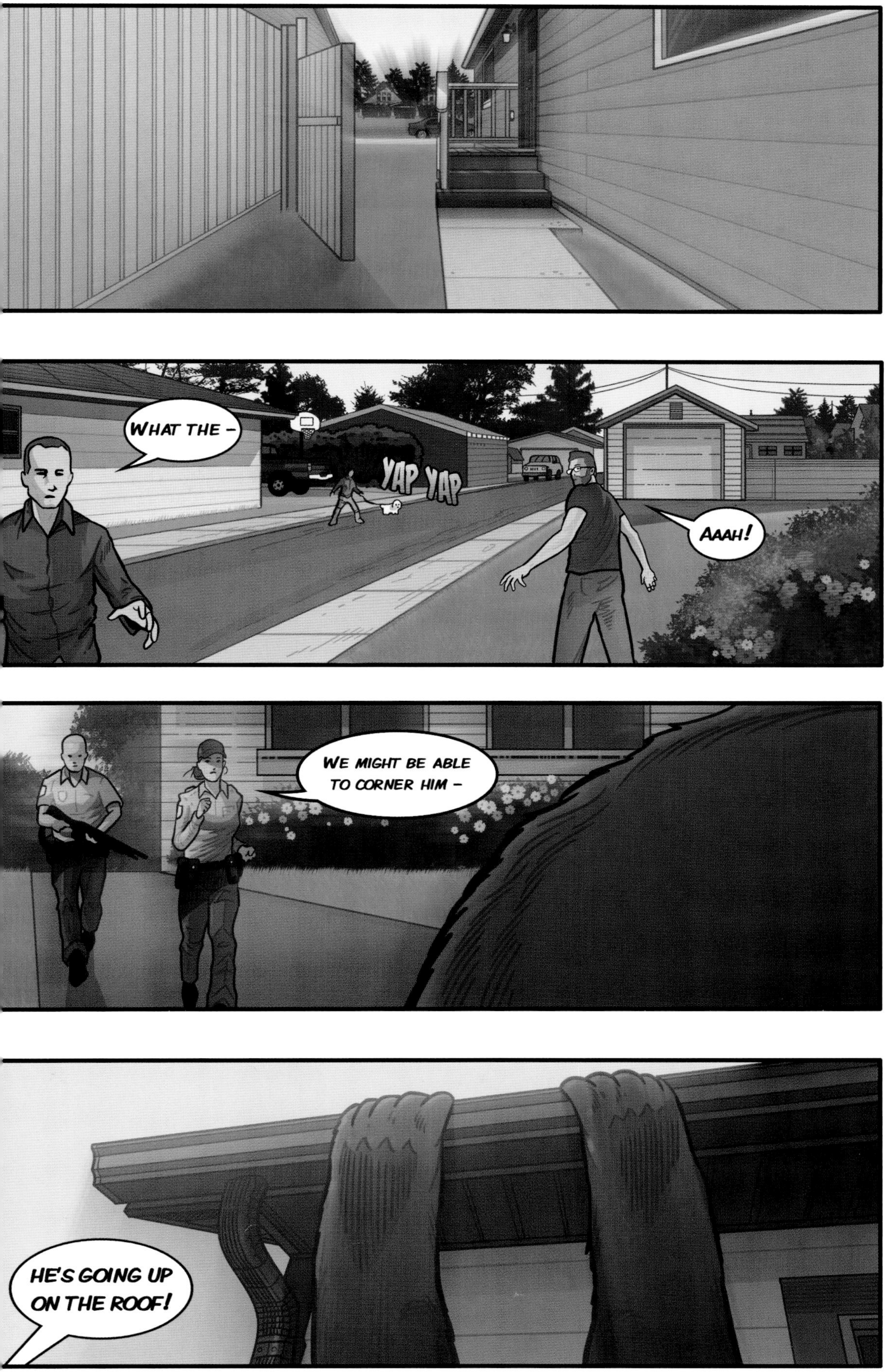
WHAT THE -
YAP YAP
AAAH!
WE MIGHT BE ABLE TO CORNER HIM -
HE'S GOING UP ON THE ROOF!

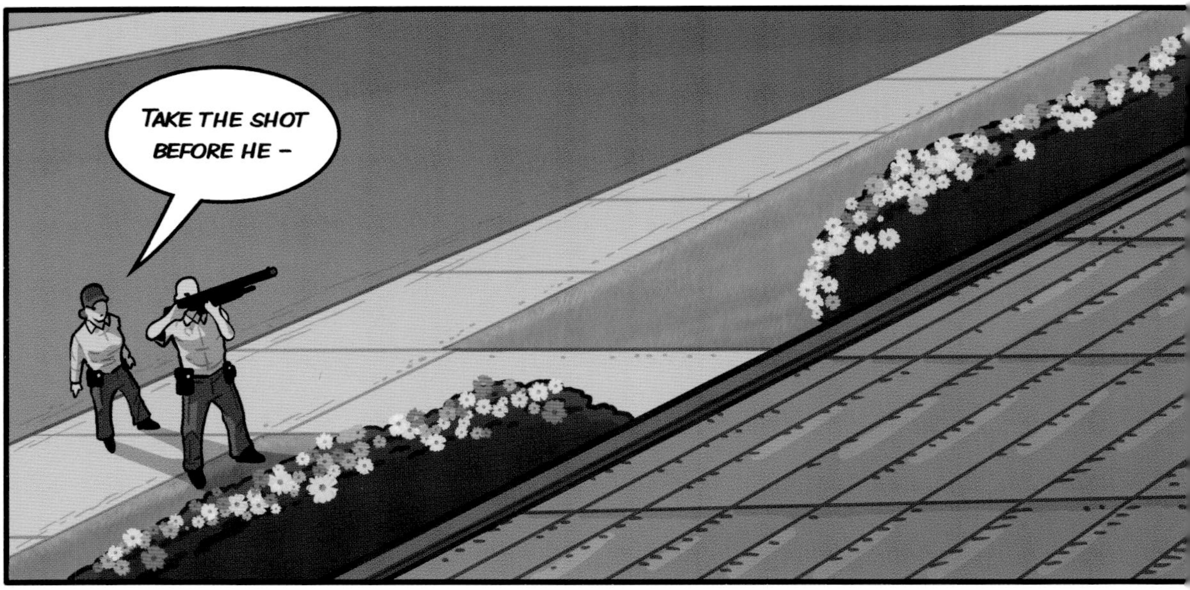
TAKE THE SHOT BEFORE HE -

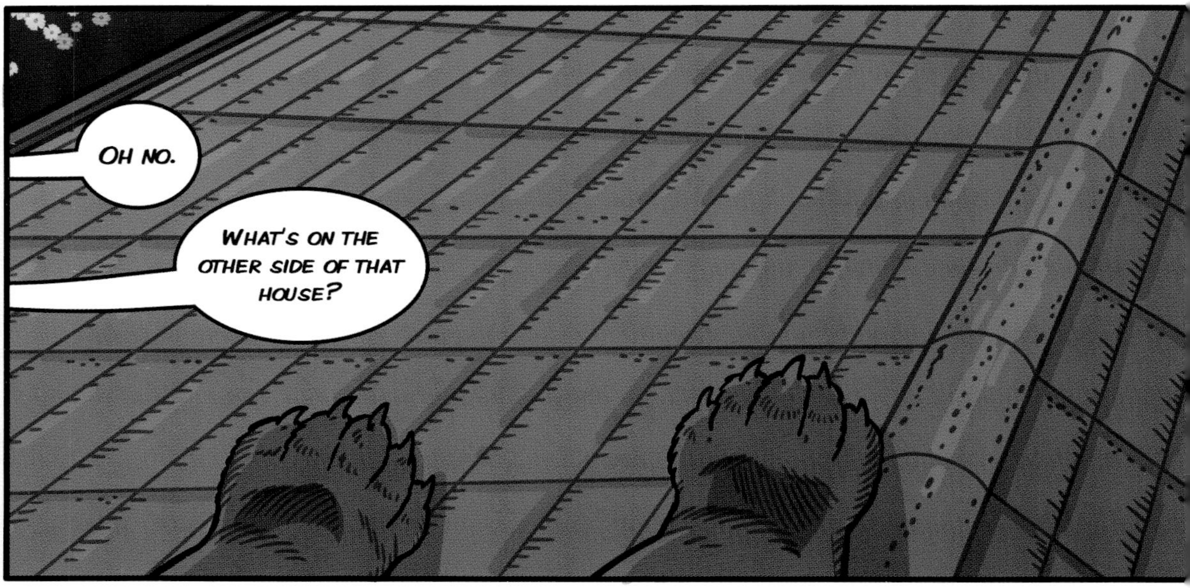
OH NO.
WHAT'S ON THE OTHER SIDE OF THAT HOUSE?

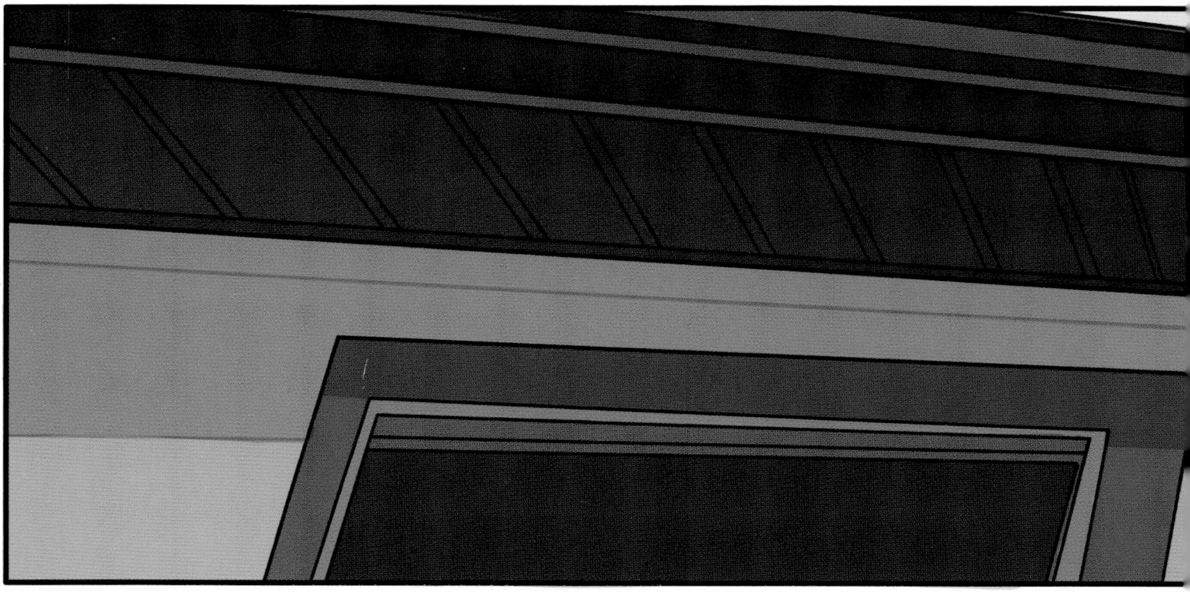

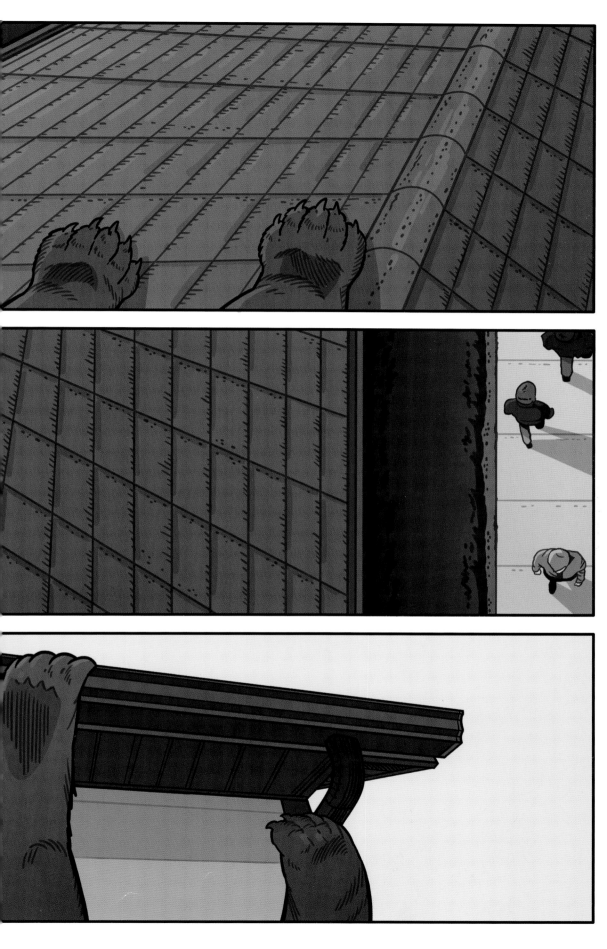

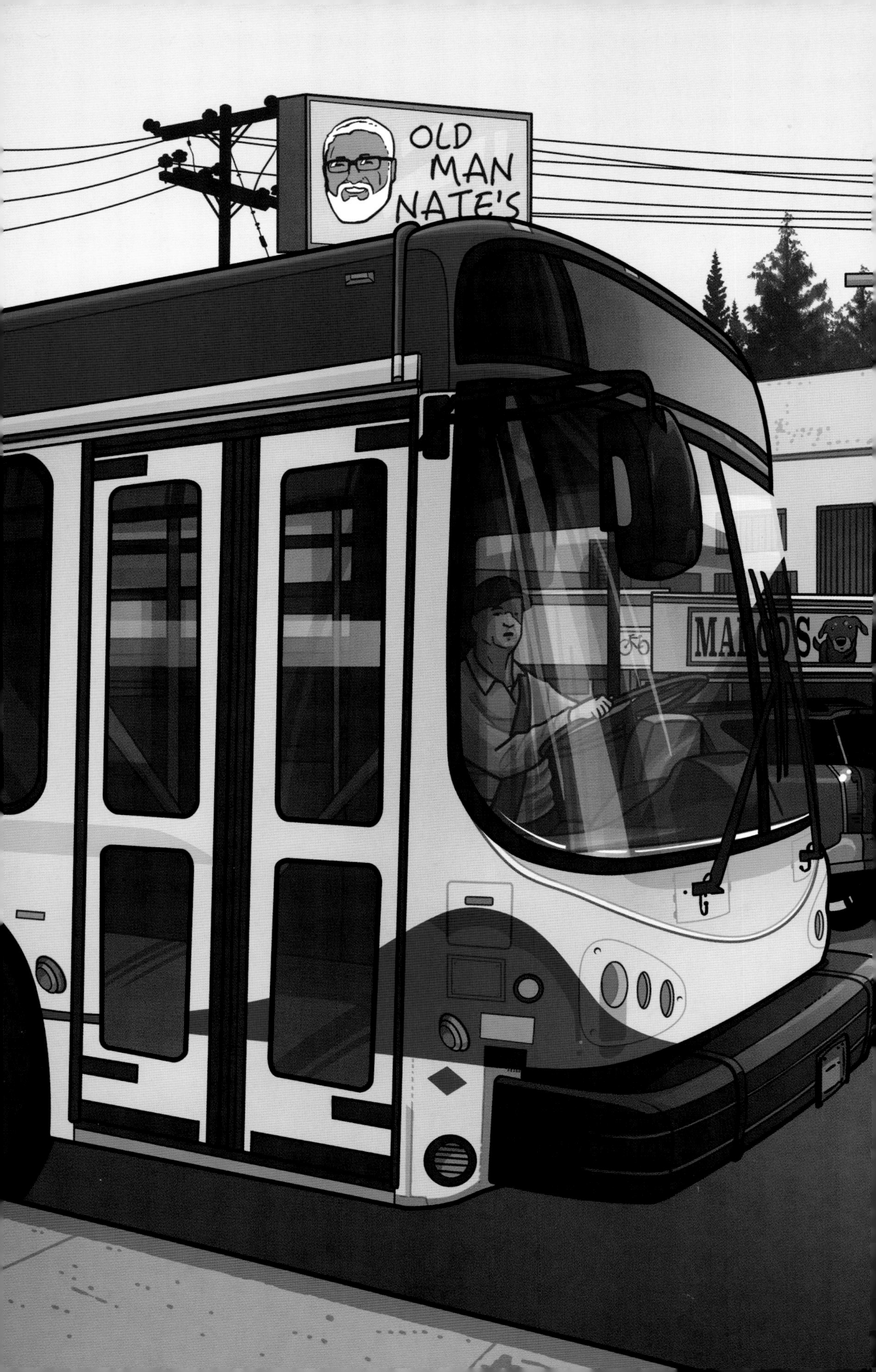
OLD MAN NATE'S

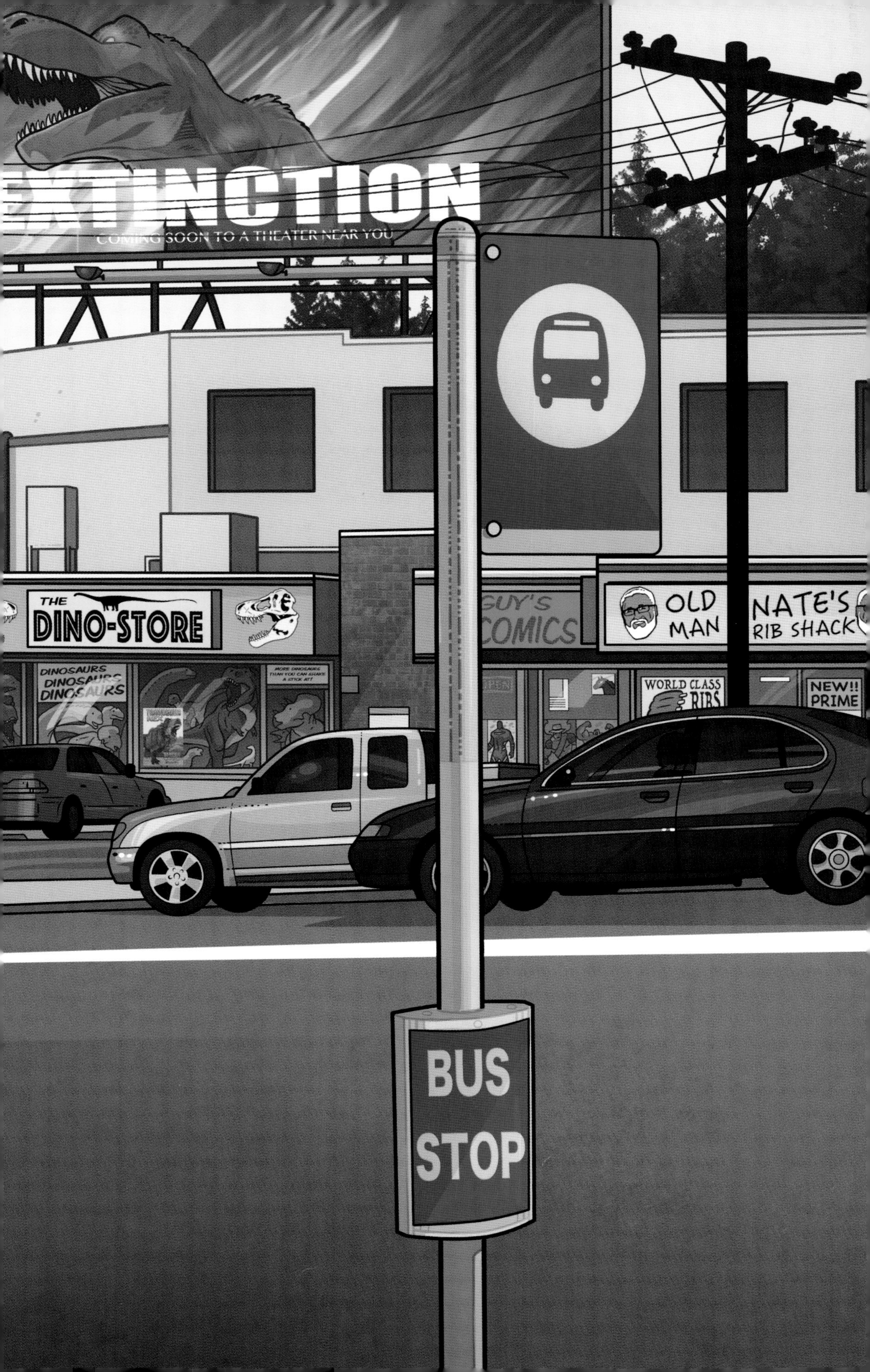
EXTINCTION
COMING SOON TO A THEATER NEAR YOU
THE DINO-STORE
DINOSAURS DINOSAURS DINOSAURS
MORE DINOSAURS THAN YOU CAN SHAKE A STICK AT!
GUY'S COMICS
OLD MAN NATE'S RIB SHACK
WORLD CLASS RIBS
NEW!! PRIME
BUS STOP

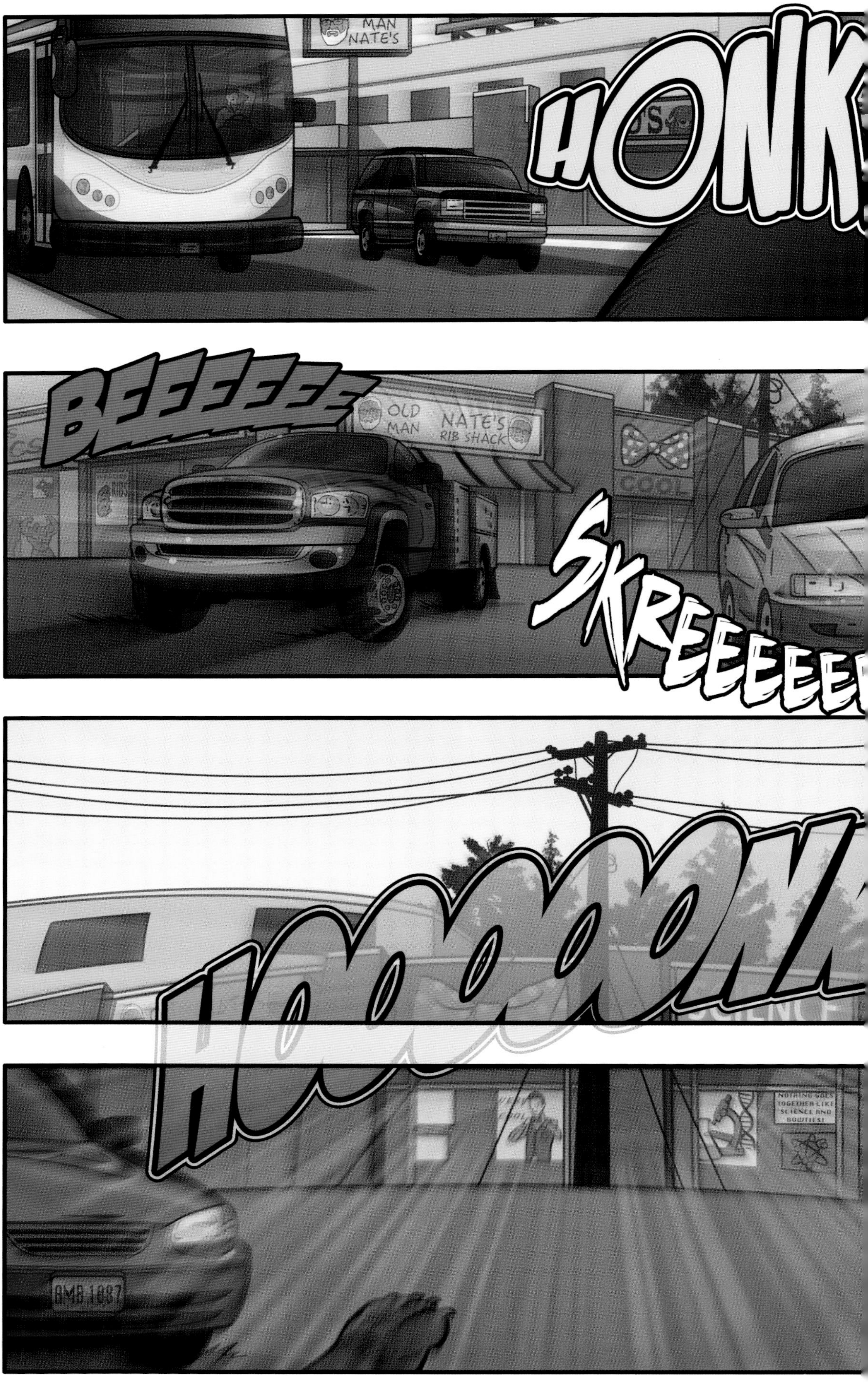
MAN NATE'S
HONK
BEEEEEE
OLD MAN NATE'S RIB SHACK
COOL
SKREEEEEE
HOOOOONK
SCIENCE
NOTHING GOES TOGETHER LIKE SCIENCE AND BOWTIES!
AMB 1087

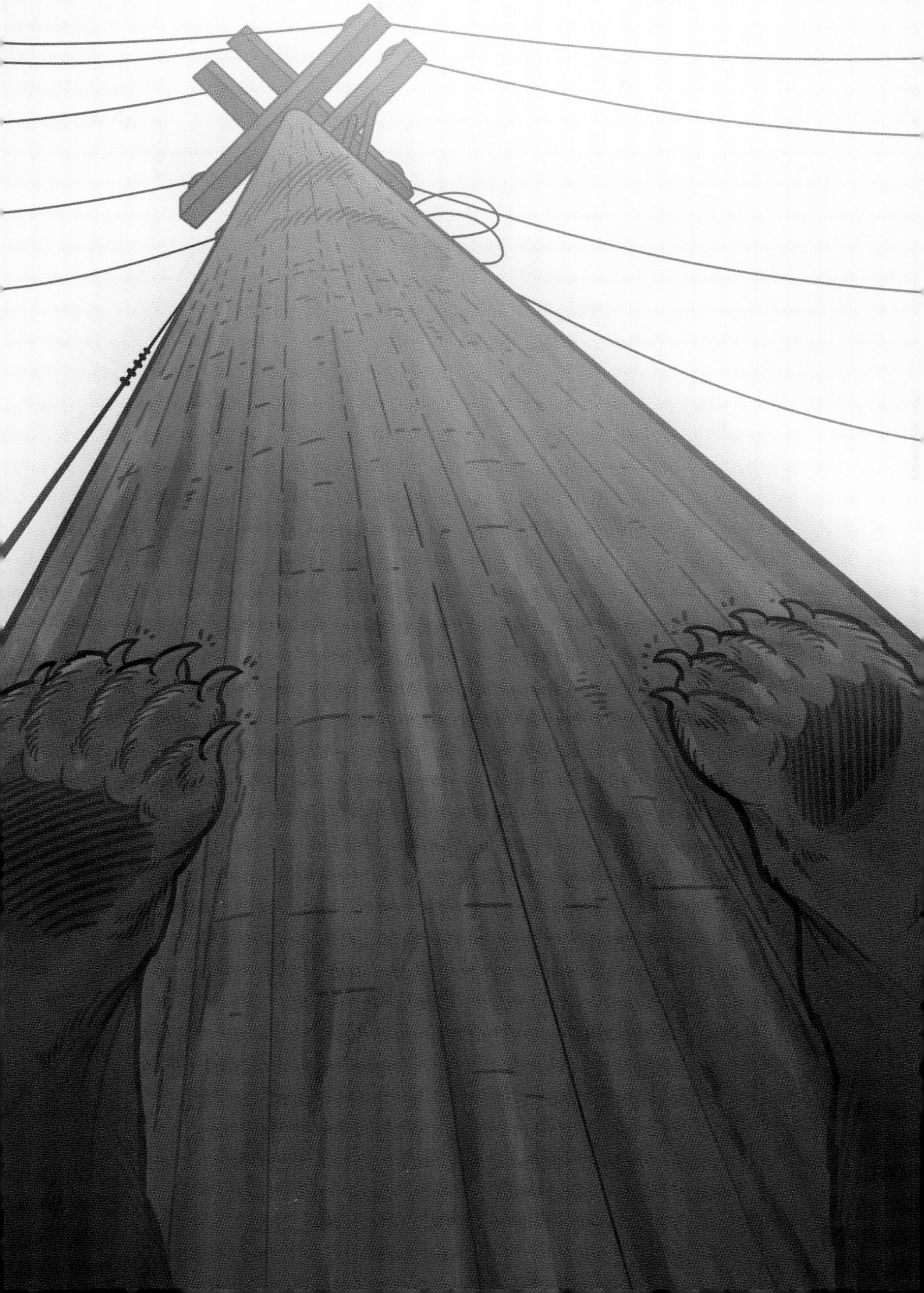

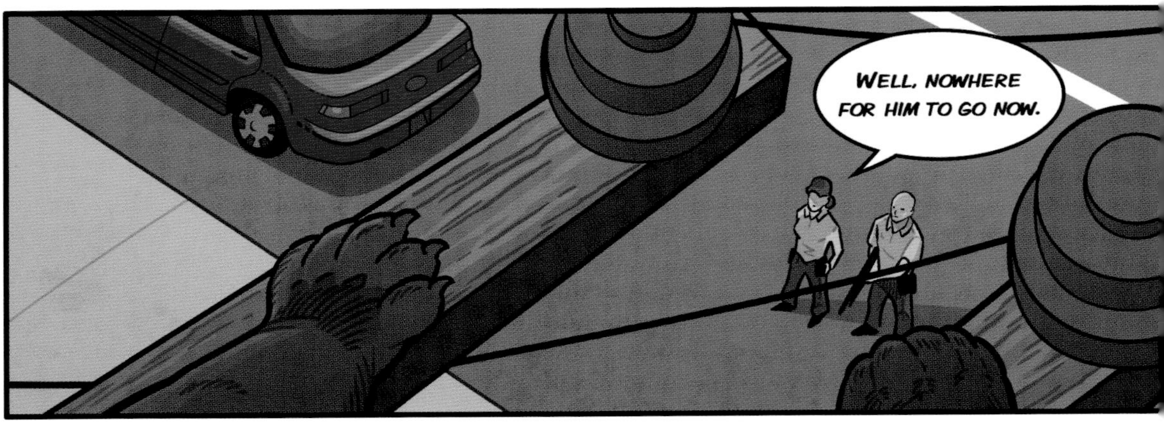
WELL, NOWHERE FOR HIM TO GO NOW.

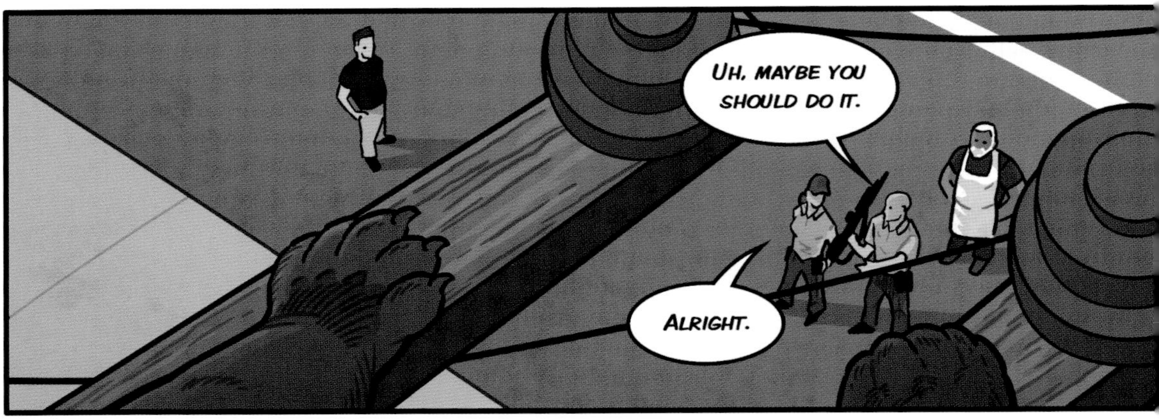
UH, MAYBE YOU SHOULD DO IT.
ALRIGHT.

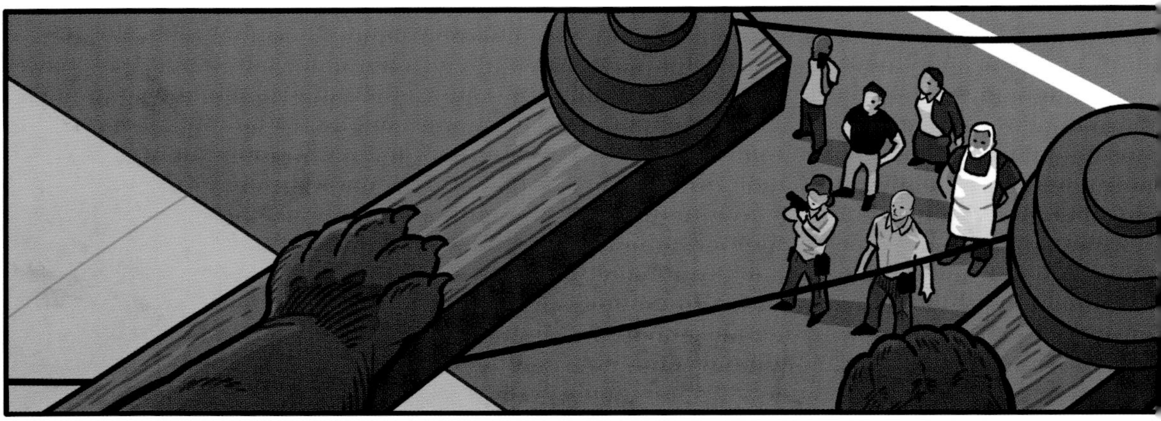

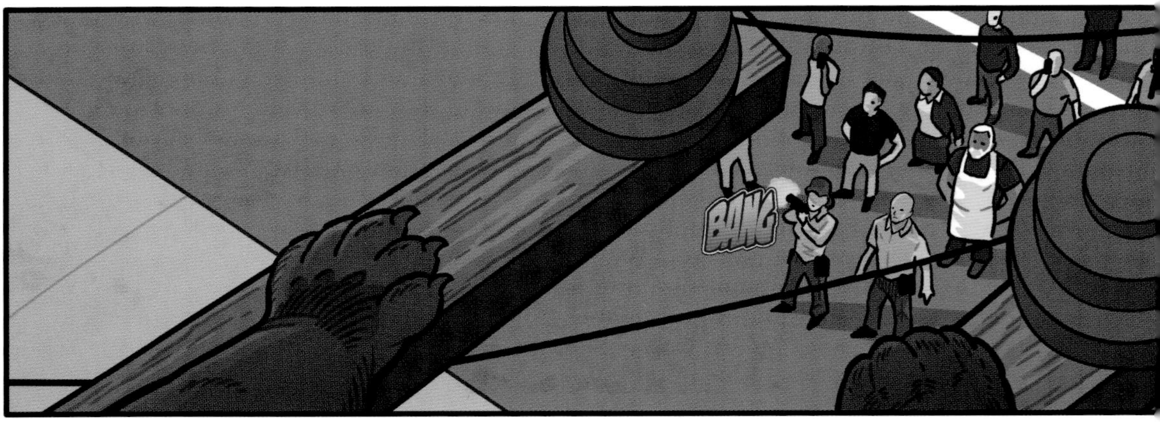
BANG

THWIP
GOT HIM!
NICE SHOT!
ALRIGHT, LET'S GET THIS MAT IN POSITION. HE'S ABOUT TO TAKE THE FAST WAY DOWN.

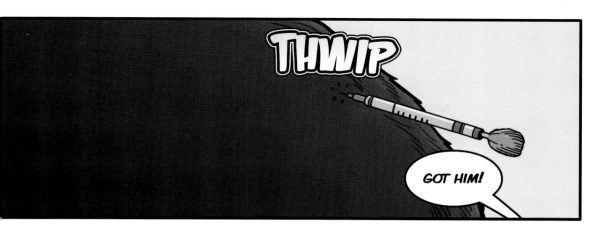

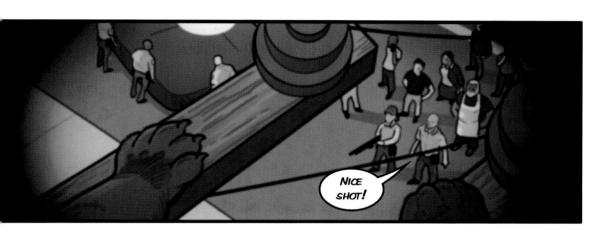

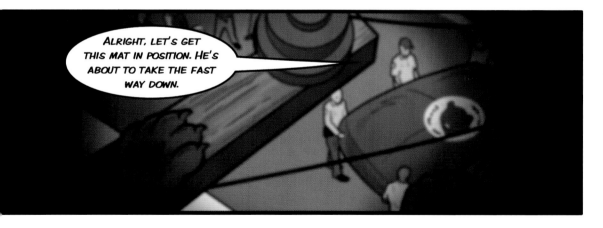

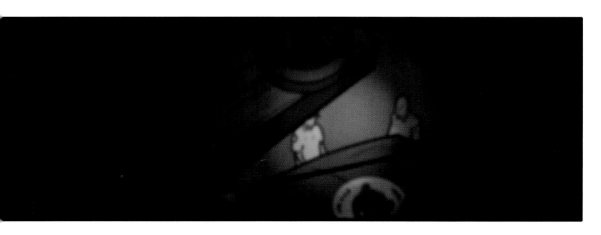

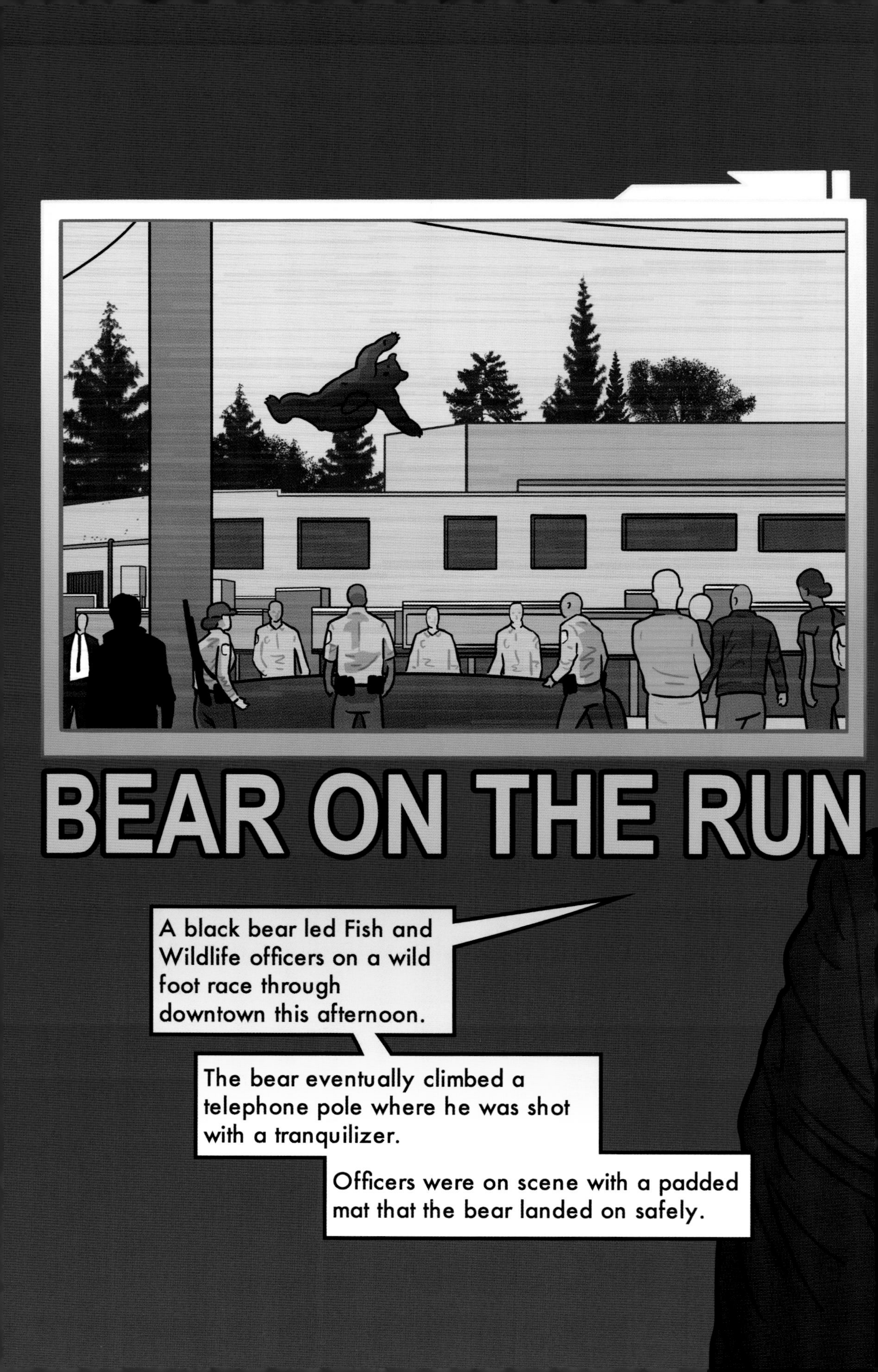
BEAR ON THE RUN
A black bear led Fish and Wildlife officers on a wild foot race through downtown this afternoon.
The bear eventually climbed a telephone pole where he was shot with a tranquilizer.
Officers were on scene with a padded mat that the bear landed on safely.

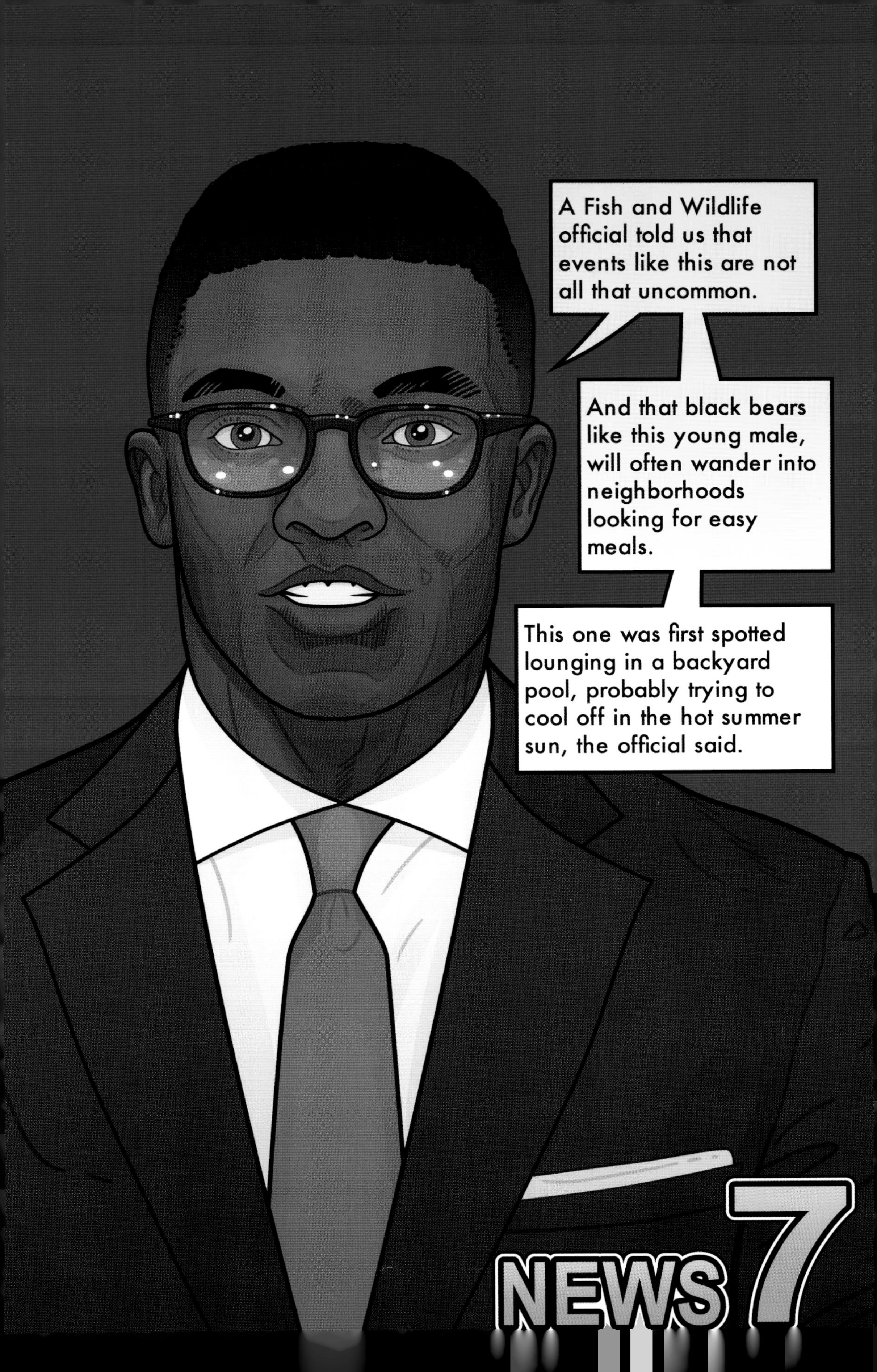
A Fish and Wildlife official told us that events like this are not all that uncommon.
And that black bears like this young male, will often wander into neighborhoods looking for easy meals.
This one was first spotted lounging in a backyard pool, probably trying to cool off in the hot summer sun, the official said.
NEWS 7

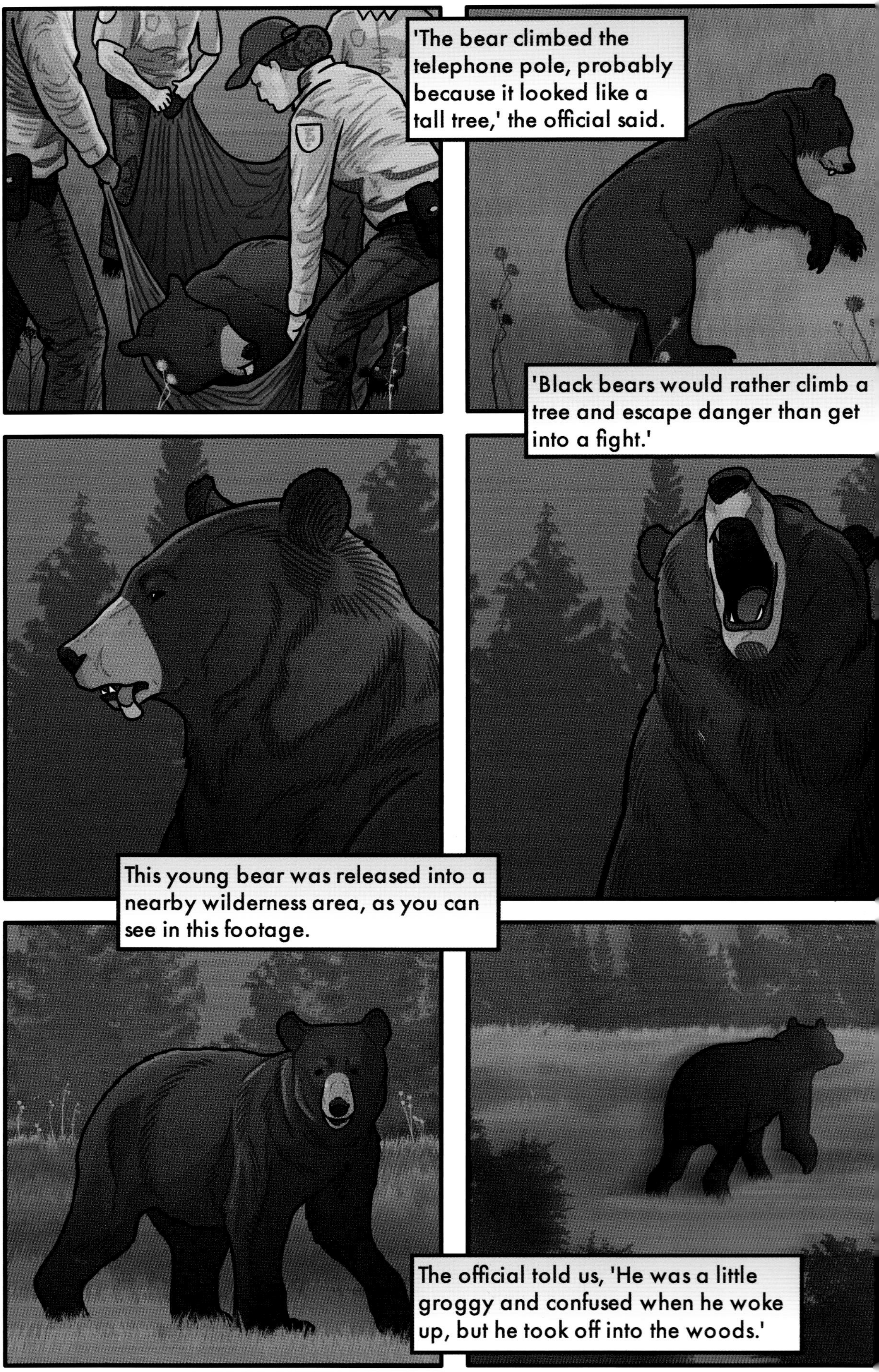
'The bear climbed the telephone pole, probably because it looked like a tall tree,' the official said.
'Black bears would rather climb a tree and escape danger than get into a fight.'
This young bear was released into a nearby wilderness area, as you can see in this footage.
The official told us, 'He was a little groggy and confused when he woke up, but he took off into the woods.'

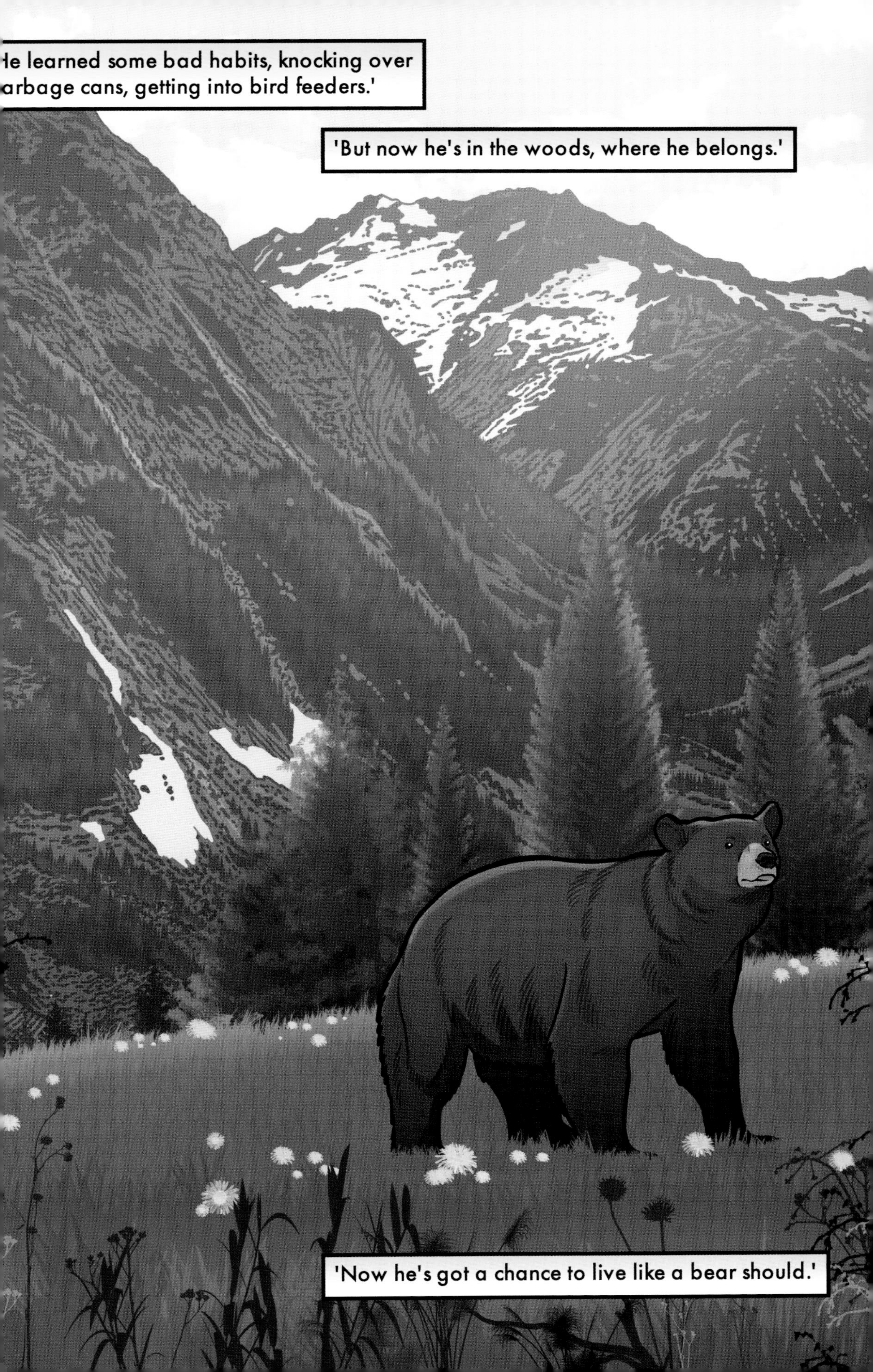

le learned some bad habits, knocking over
arbage cans, getting into bird feeders.'
'But now he's in the woods, where he belongs.'
'Now he's got a chance to live like a bear should.'

POLAR BEAR

URSUS MARITIMUS

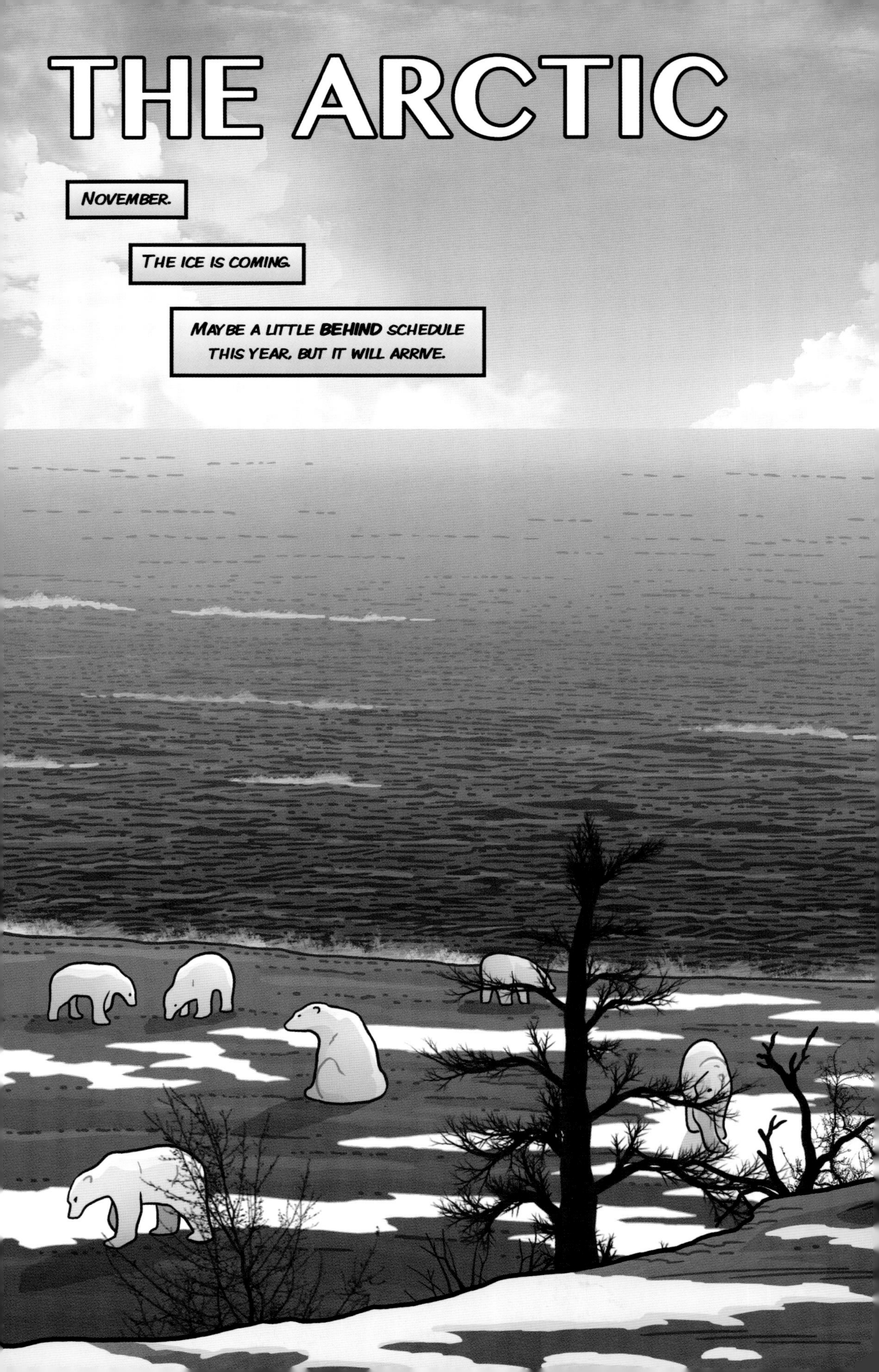
THE ARCTIC
NOVEMBER.
THE ICE IS COMING.
MAYBE A LITTLE BEHIND SCHEDULE THIS YEAR, BUT IT WILL ARRIVE.

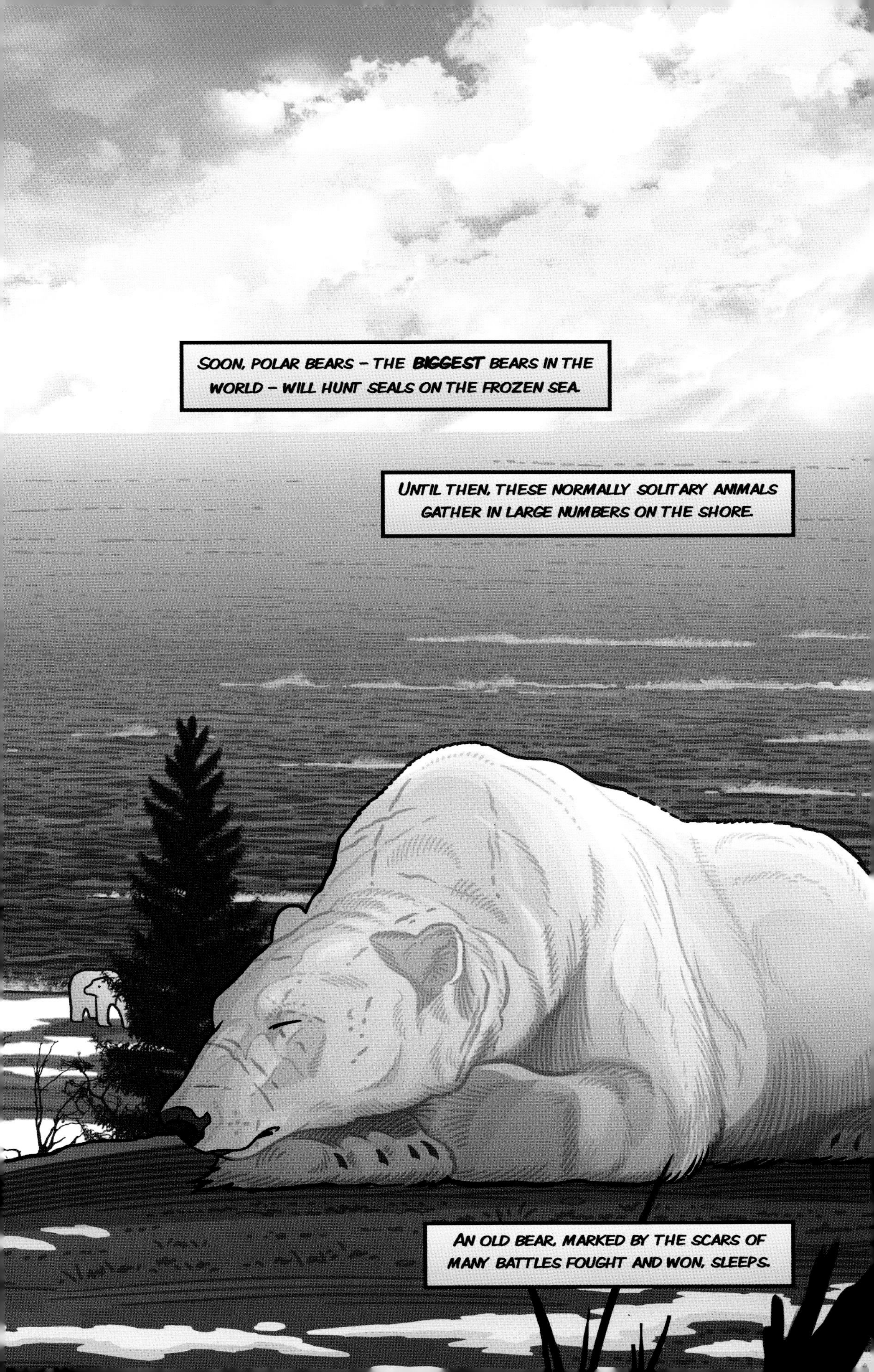
SOON, POLAR BEARS – THE **BIGGEST** BEARS IN THE WORLD – WILL HUNT SEALS ON THE FROZEN SEA.
UNTIL THEN, THESE NORMALLY SOLITARY ANIMALS GATHER IN LARGE NUMBERS ON THE SHORE.
AN OLD BEAR, MARKED BY THE SCARS OF MANY BATTLES FOUGHT AND WON, SLEEPS.

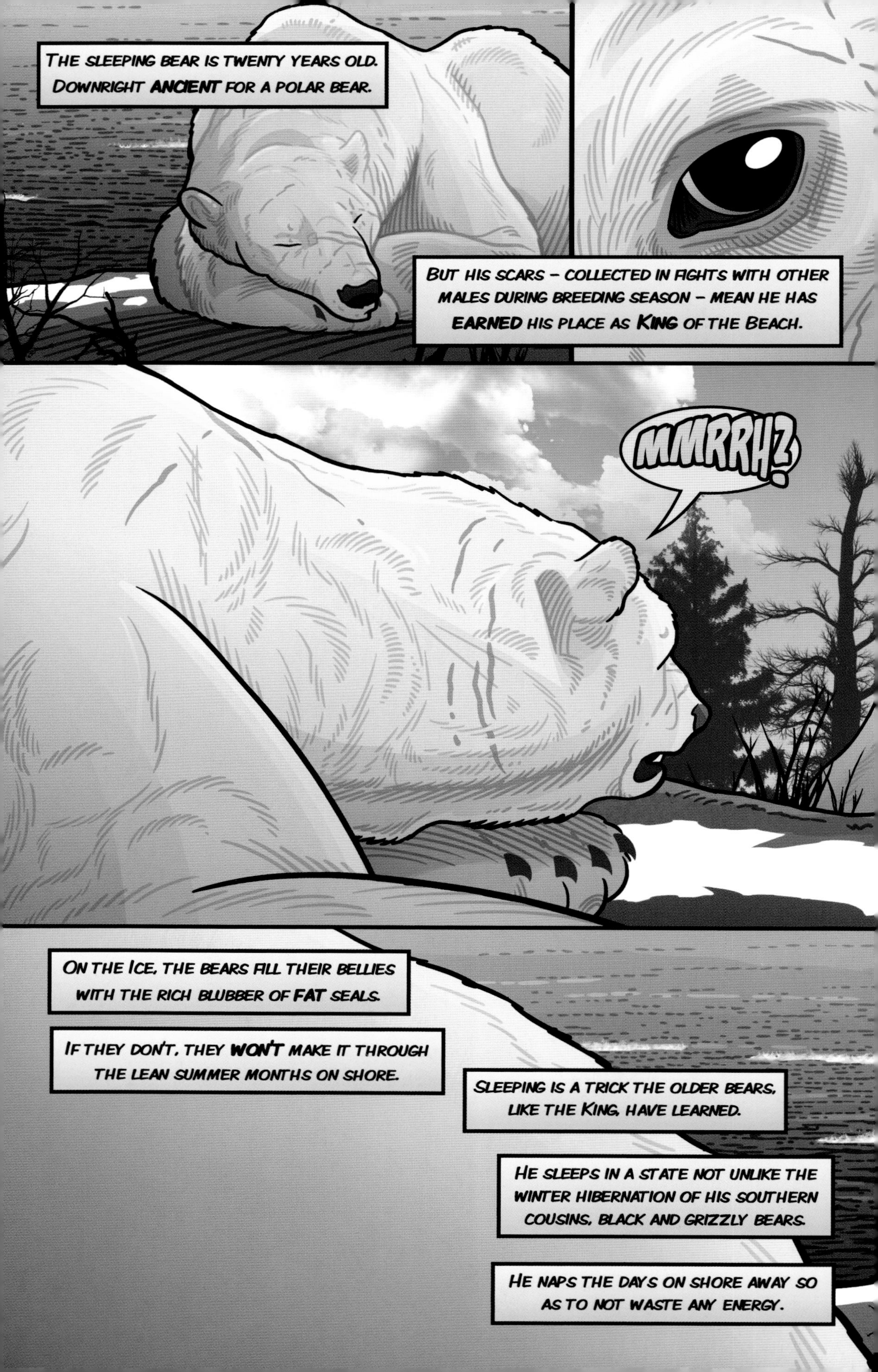
THE SLEEPING BEAR IS TWENTY YEARS OLD. DOWNRIGHT ANCIENT FOR A POLAR BEAR.
BUT HIS SCARS – COLLECTED IN FIGHTS WITH OTHER MALES DURING BREEDING SEASON – MEAN HE HAS EARNED HIS PLACE AS KING OF THE BEACH.
MMRRHZ
ON THE ICE, THE BEARS FILL THEIR BELLIES WITH THE RICH BLUBBER OF FAT SEALS.
IF THEY DON'T, THEY WON'T MAKE IT THROUGH THE LEAN SUMMER MONTHS ON SHORE.
SLEEPING IS A TRICK THE OLDER BEARS, LIKE THE KING, HAVE LEARNED.
HE SLEEPS IN A STATE NOT UNLIKE THE WINTER HIBERNATION OF HIS SOUTHERN COUSINS, BLACK AND GRIZZLY BEARS.
HE NAPS THE DAYS ON SHORE AWAY SO AS TO NOT WASTE ANY ENERGY.

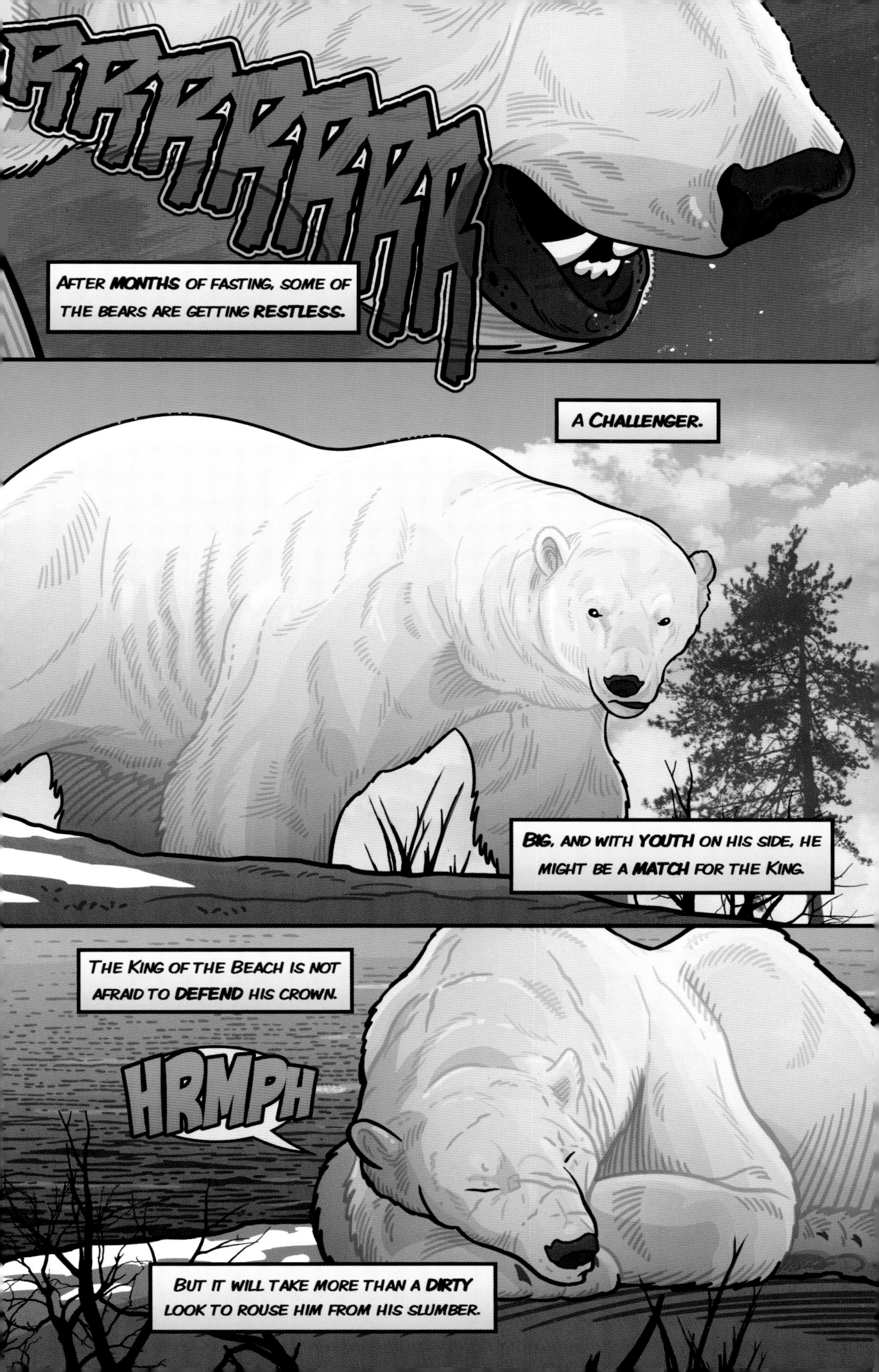
RRRRRRRR
AFTER MONTHS OF FASTING, SOME OF THE BEARS ARE GETTING RESTLESS.
A CHALLENGER.
BIG, AND WITH YOUTH ON HIS SIDE, HE MIGHT BE A MATCH FOR THE KING.
THE KING OF THE BEACH IS NOT AFRAID TO DEFEND HIS CROWN.
HRMPH
BUT IT WILL TAKE MORE THAN A DIRTY LOOK TO ROUSE HIM FROM HIS SLUMBER.

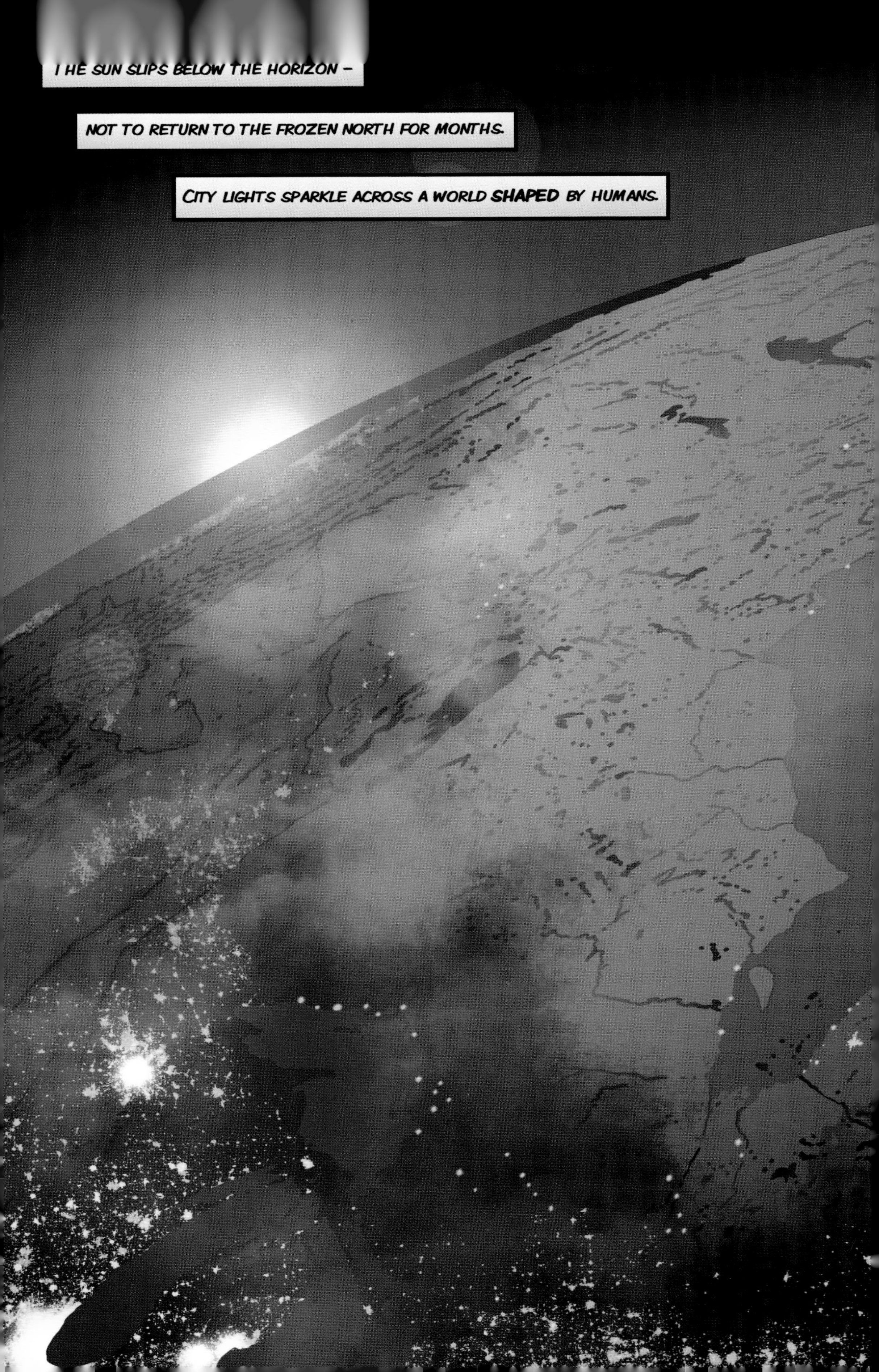
THE SUN SLIPS BELOW THE HORIZON –
NOT TO RETURN TO THE FROZEN NORTH FOR MONTHS.
CITY LIGHTS SPARKLE ACROSS A WORLD SHAPED BY HUMANS.

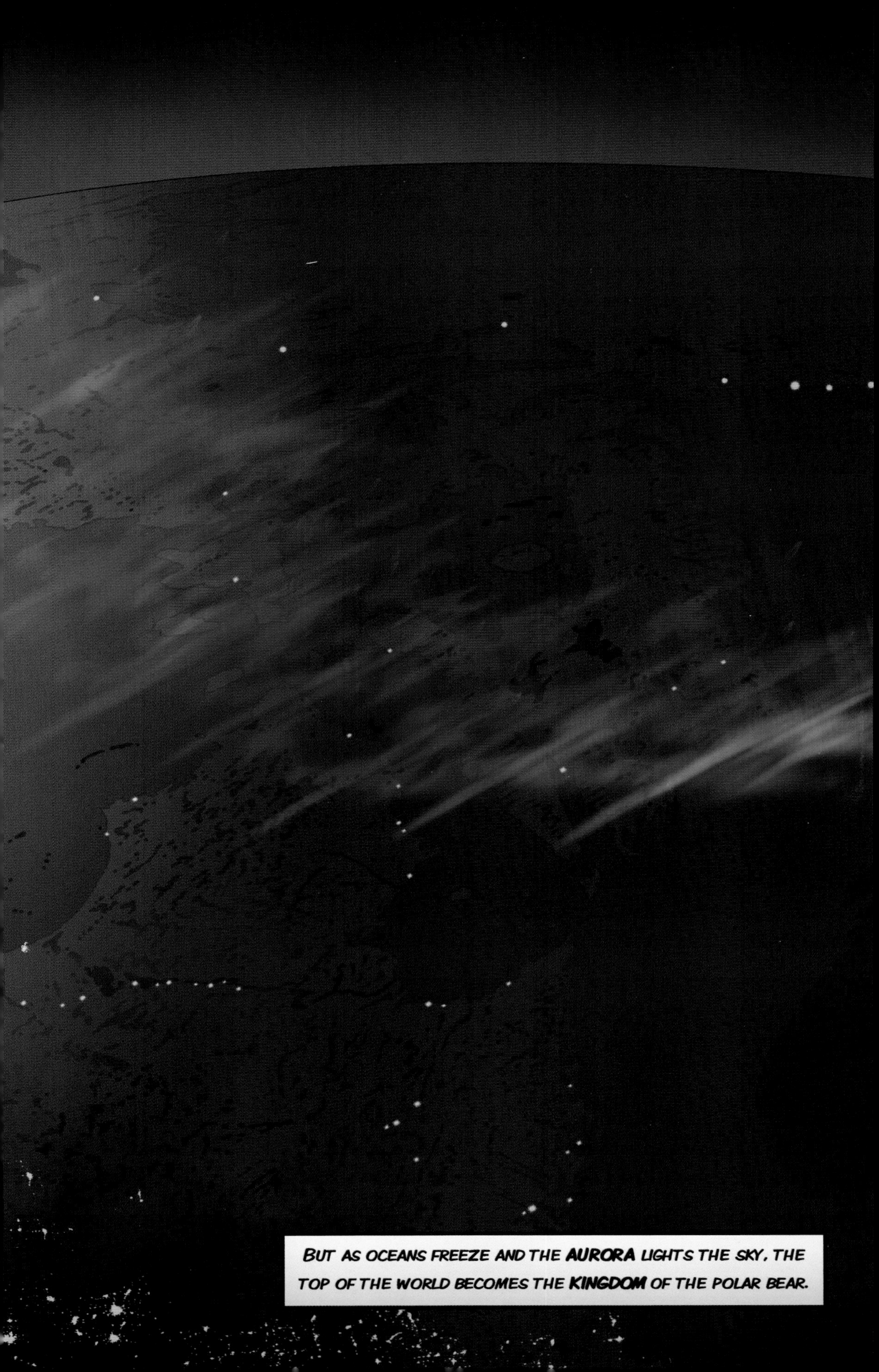
BUT AS OCEANS FREEZE AND THE AURORA LIGHTS THE SKY, THE TOP OF THE WORLD BECOMES THE KINGDOM OF THE POLAR BEAR.

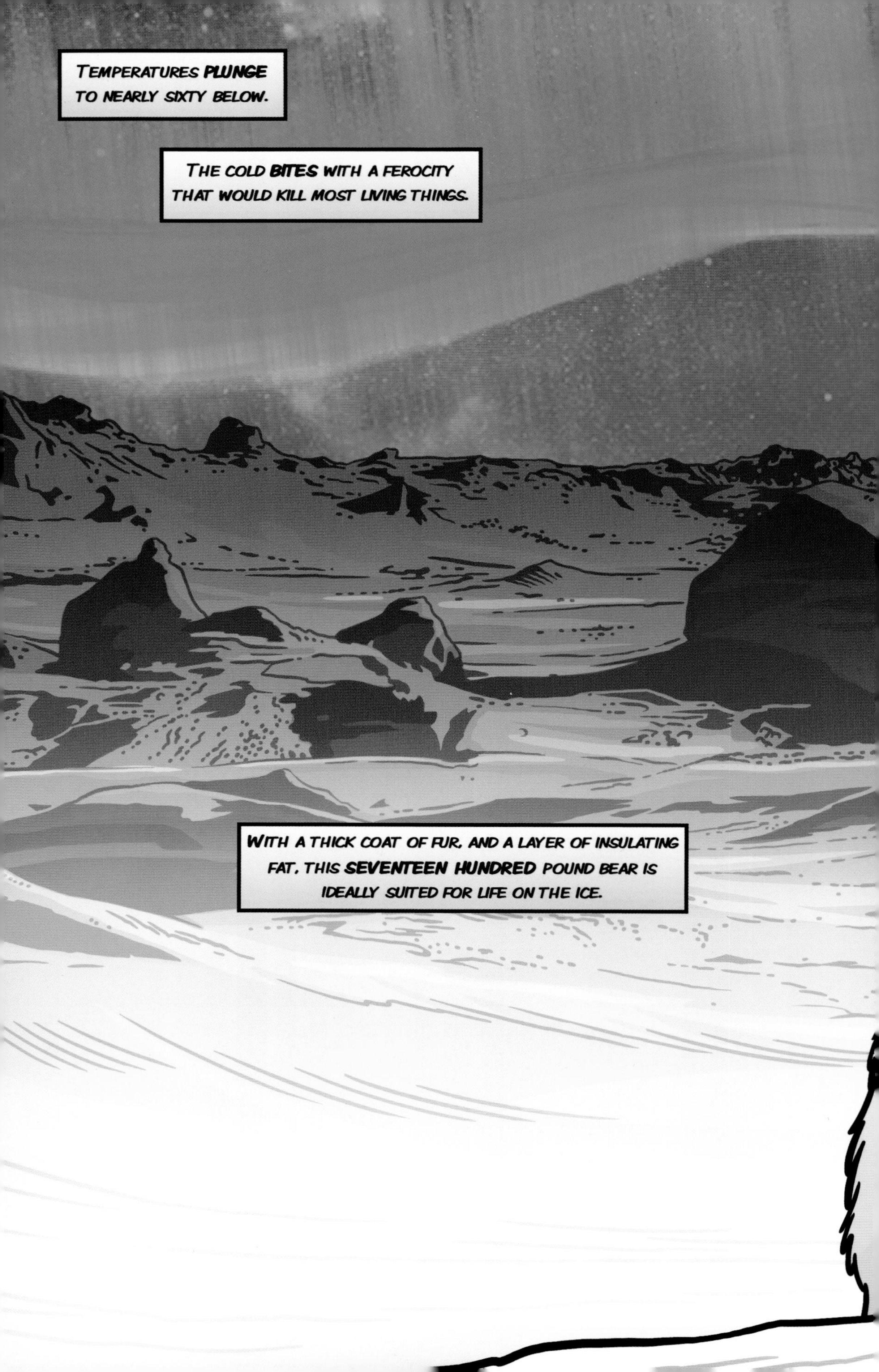
TEMPERATURES PLUNGE TO NEARLY SIXTY BELOW.
THE COLD BITES WITH A FEROCITY THAT WOULD KILL MOST LIVING THINGS.
WITH A THICK COAT OF FUR, AND A LAYER OF INSULATING FAT, THIS SEVENTEEN HUNDRED POUND BEAR IS IDEALLY SUITED FOR LIFE ON THE ICE.

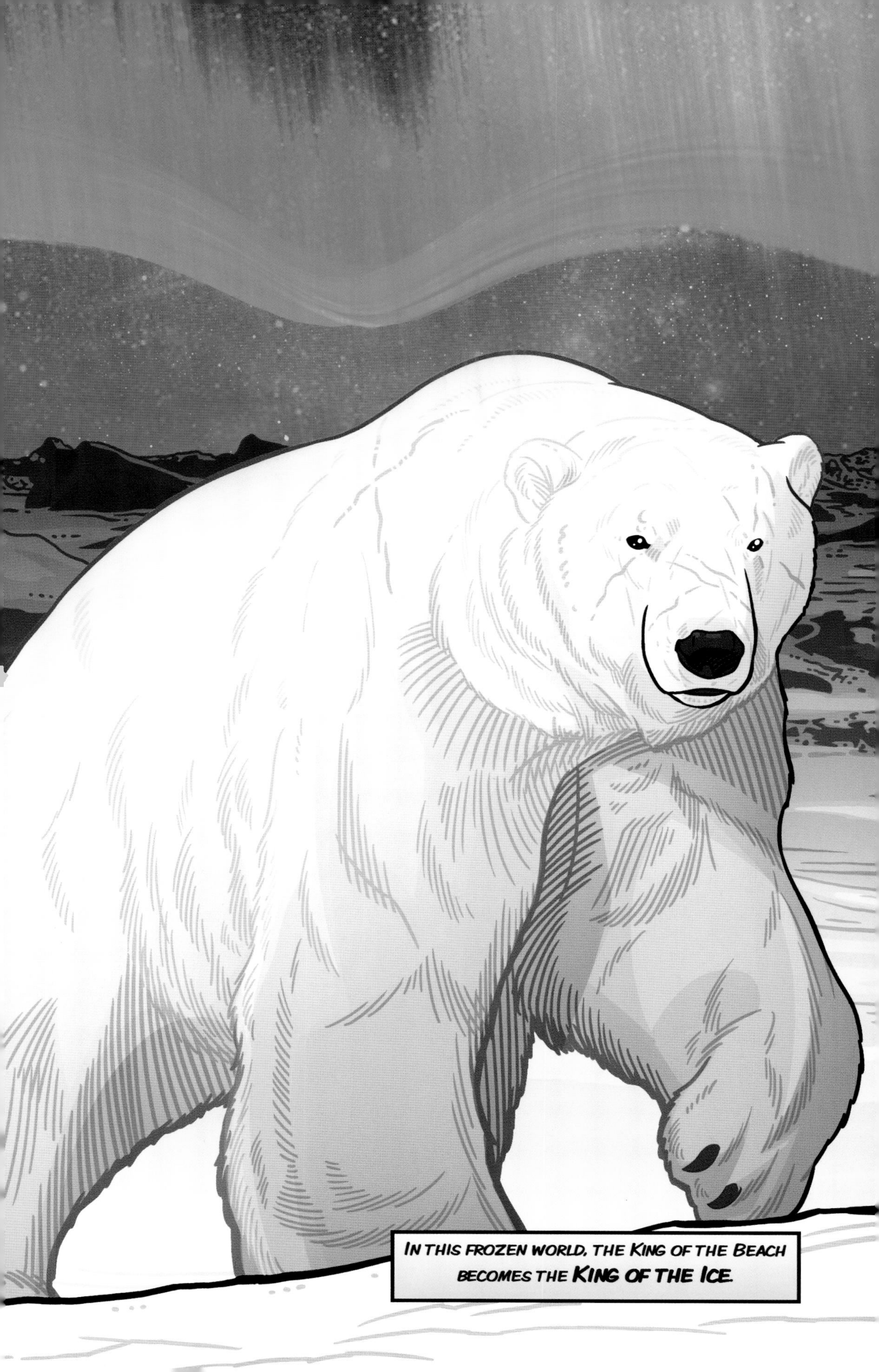
IN THIS FROZEN WORLD, THE KING OF THE BEACH BECOMES THE KING OF THE ICE.

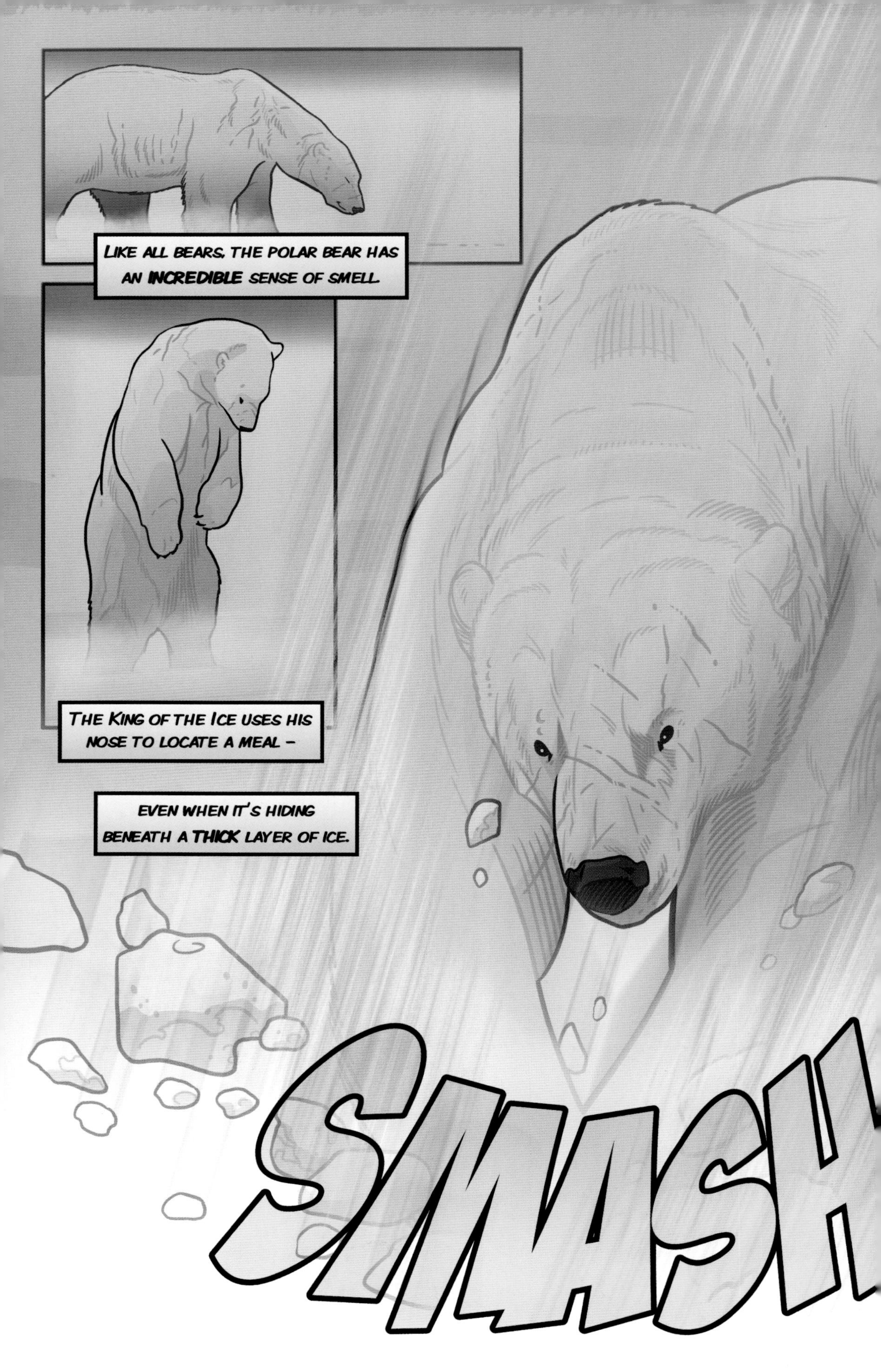
LIKE ALL BEARS, THE POLAR BEAR HAS AN INCREDIBLE SENSE OF SMELL.
THE KING OF THE ICE USES HIS NOSE TO LOCATE A MEAL –
EVEN WHEN IT'S HIDING BENEATH A THICK LAYER OF ICE.
SMASH

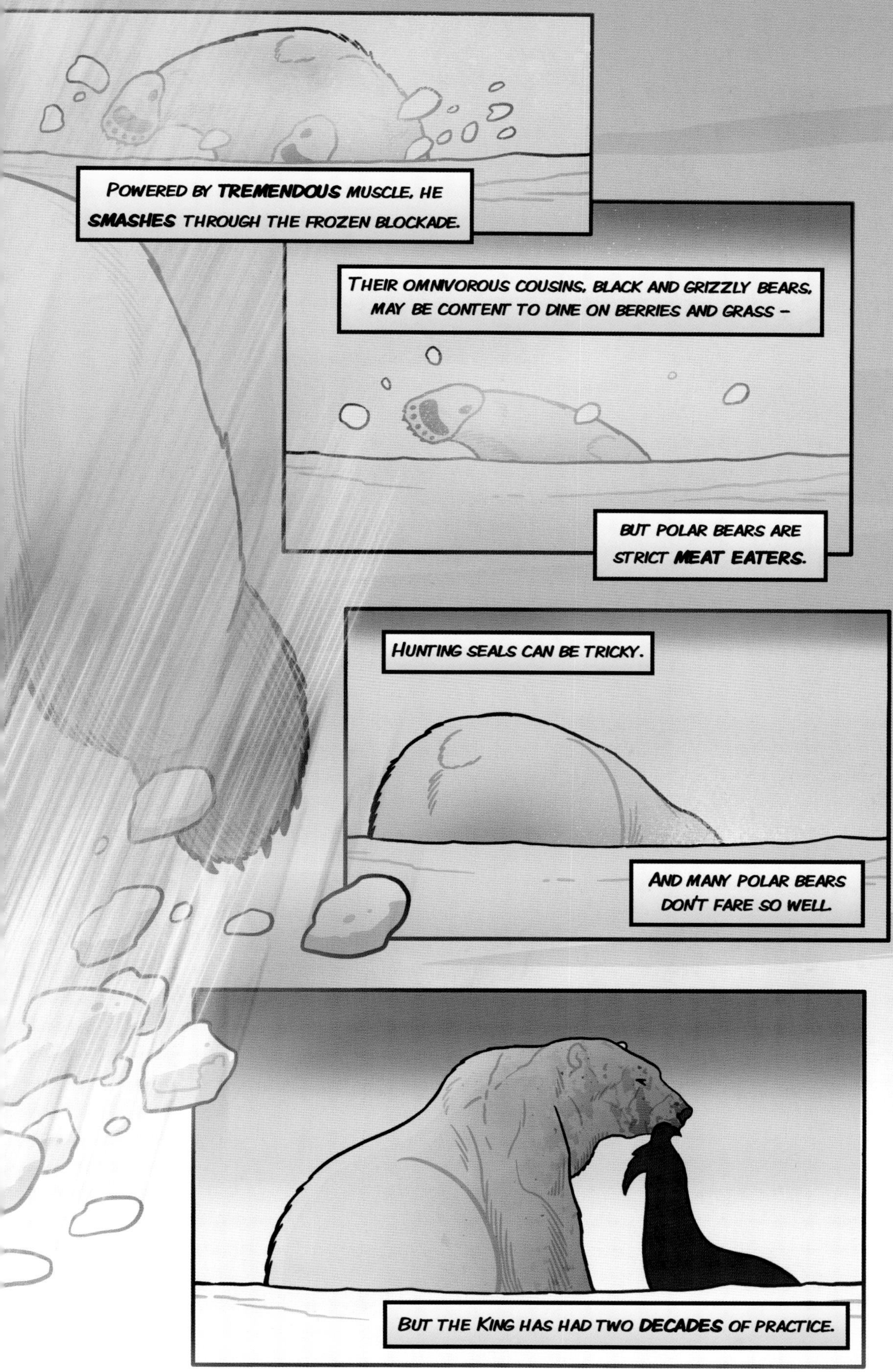
POWERED BY TREMENDOUS MUSCLE, HE SMASHES THROUGH THE FROZEN BLOCKADE.
THEIR OMNIVOROUS COUSINS, BLACK AND GRIZZLY BEARS, MAY BE CONTENT TO DINE ON BERRIES AND GRASS –
BUT POLAR BEARS ARE STRICT MEAT EATERS.
HUNTING SEALS CAN BE TRICKY.
AND MANY POLAR BEARS DON'T FARE SO WELL.
BUT THE KING HAS HAD TWO DECADES OF PRACTICE.

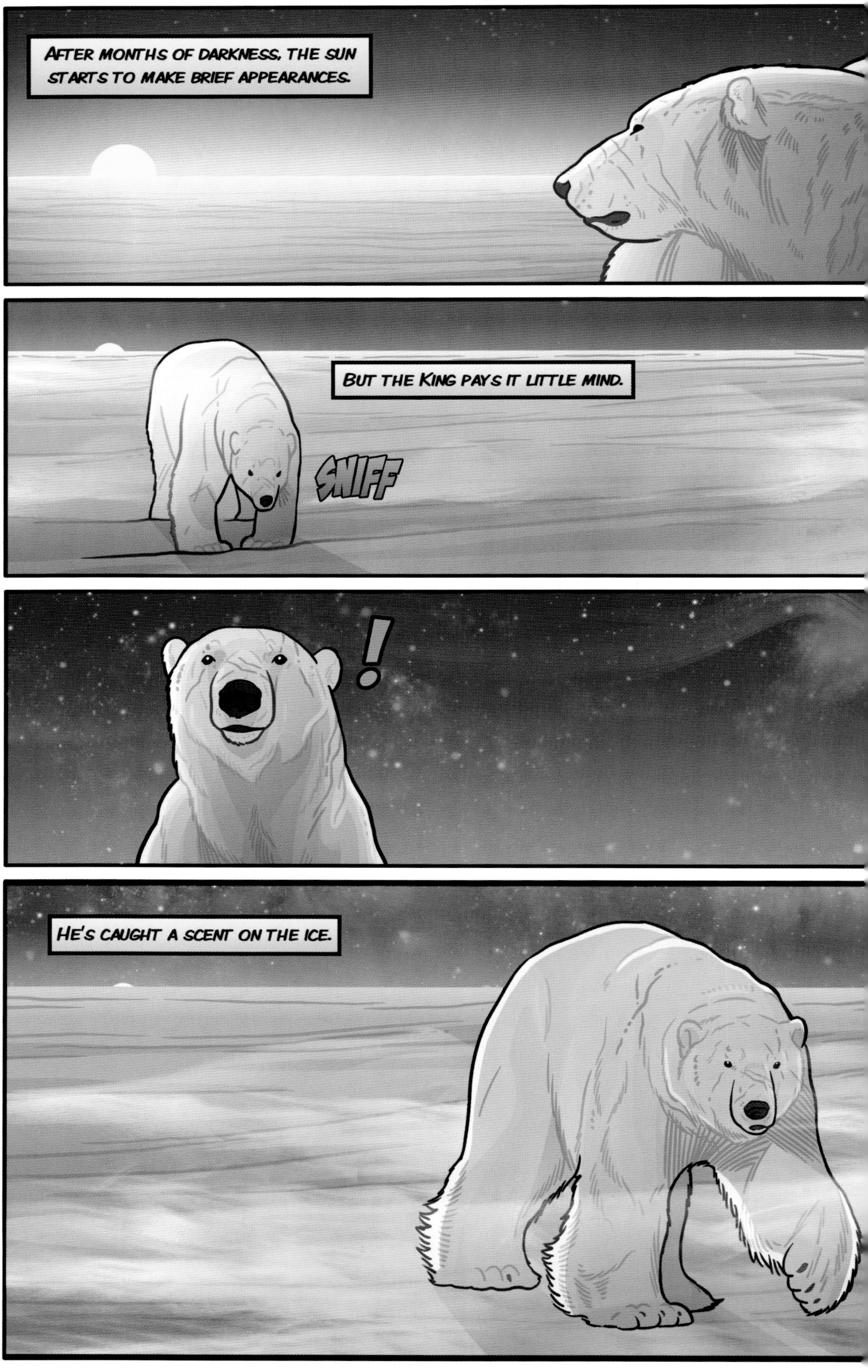
AFTER MONTHS OF DARKNESS, THE SUN STARTS TO MAKE BRIEF APPEARANCES.
BUT THE KING PAYS IT LITTLE MIND.
SNIFF
!
HE'S CAUGHT A SCENT ON THE ICE.

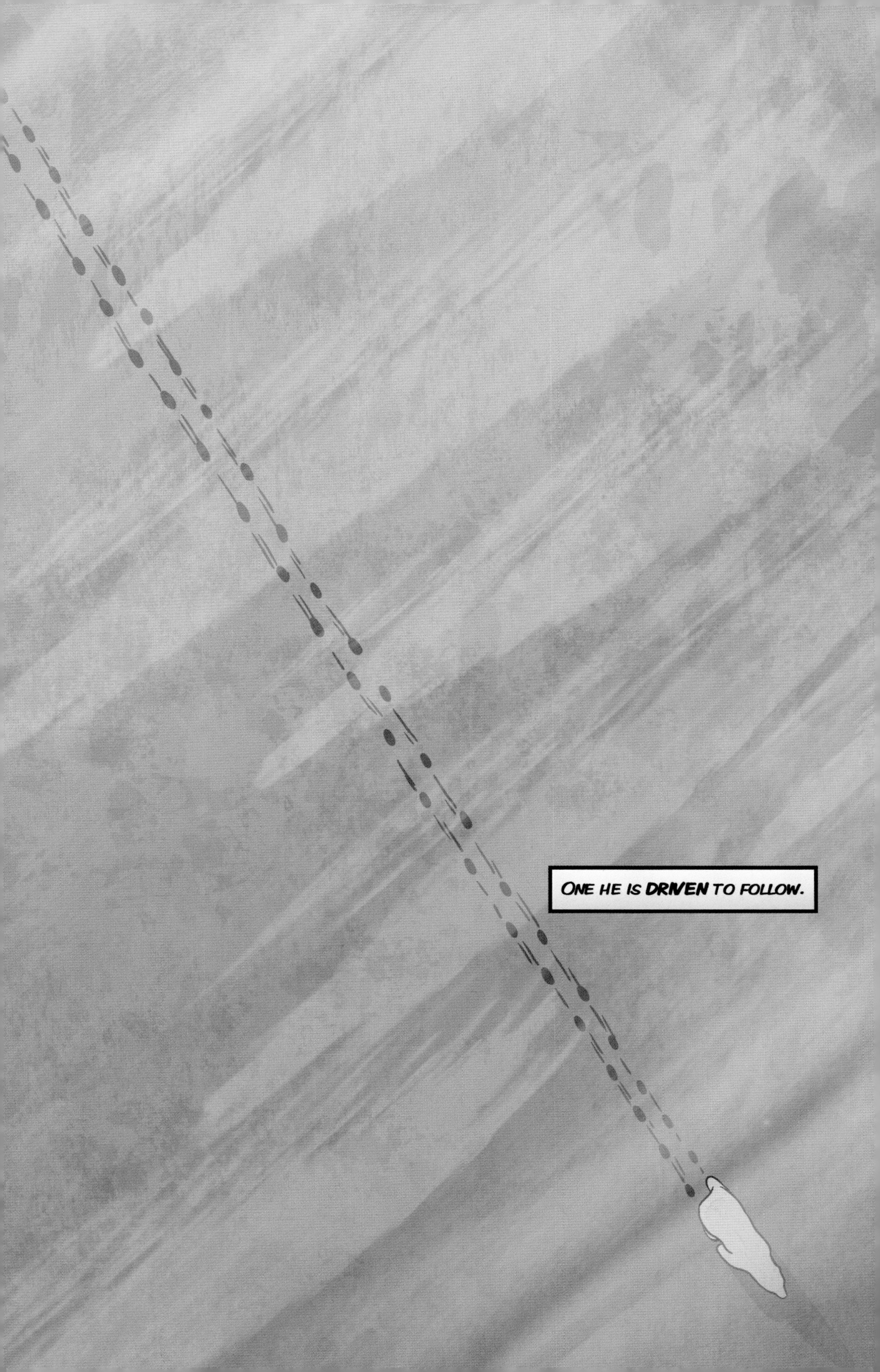
ONE HE IS DRIVEN TO FOLLOW.

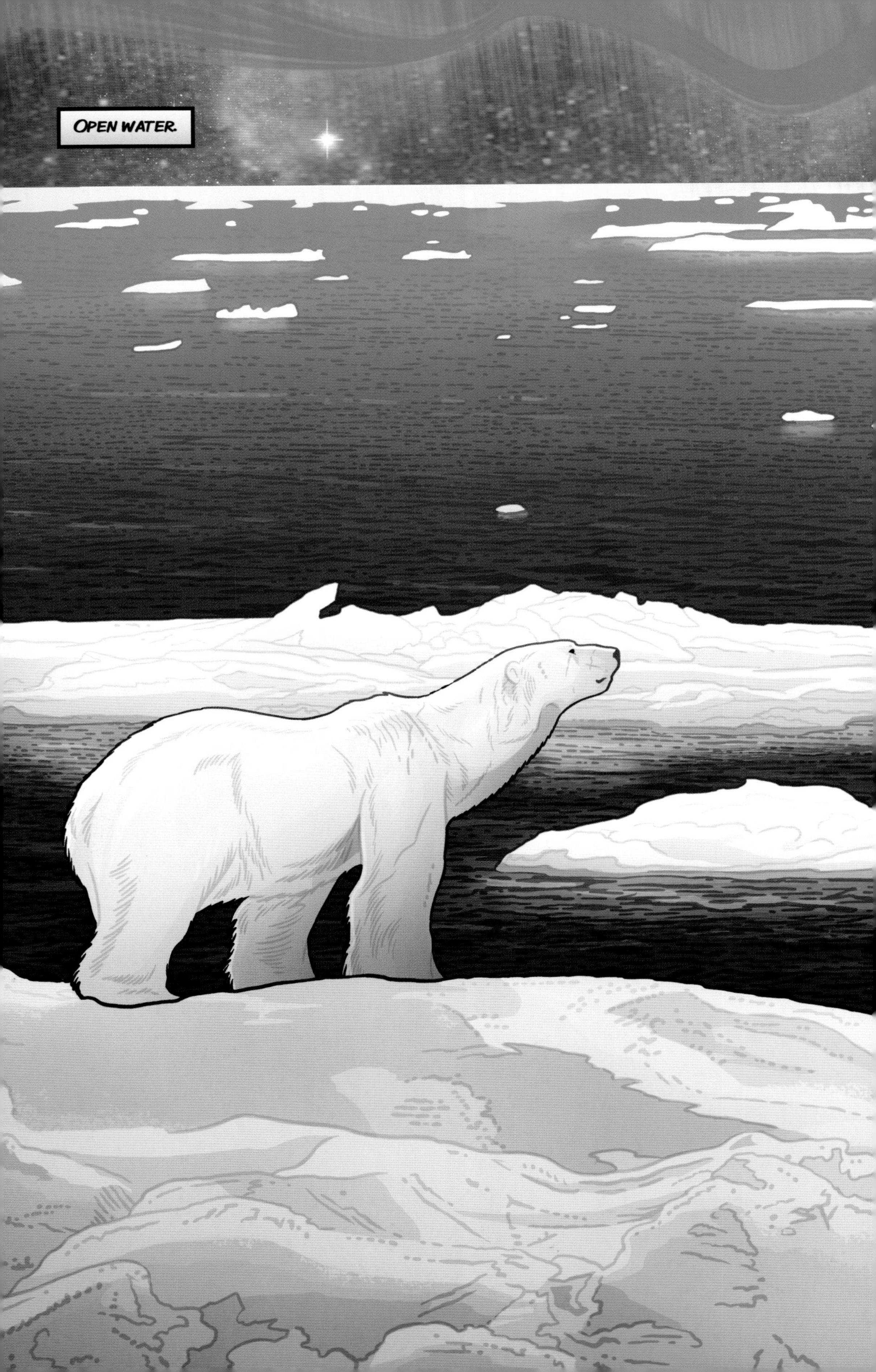
OPEN WATER.

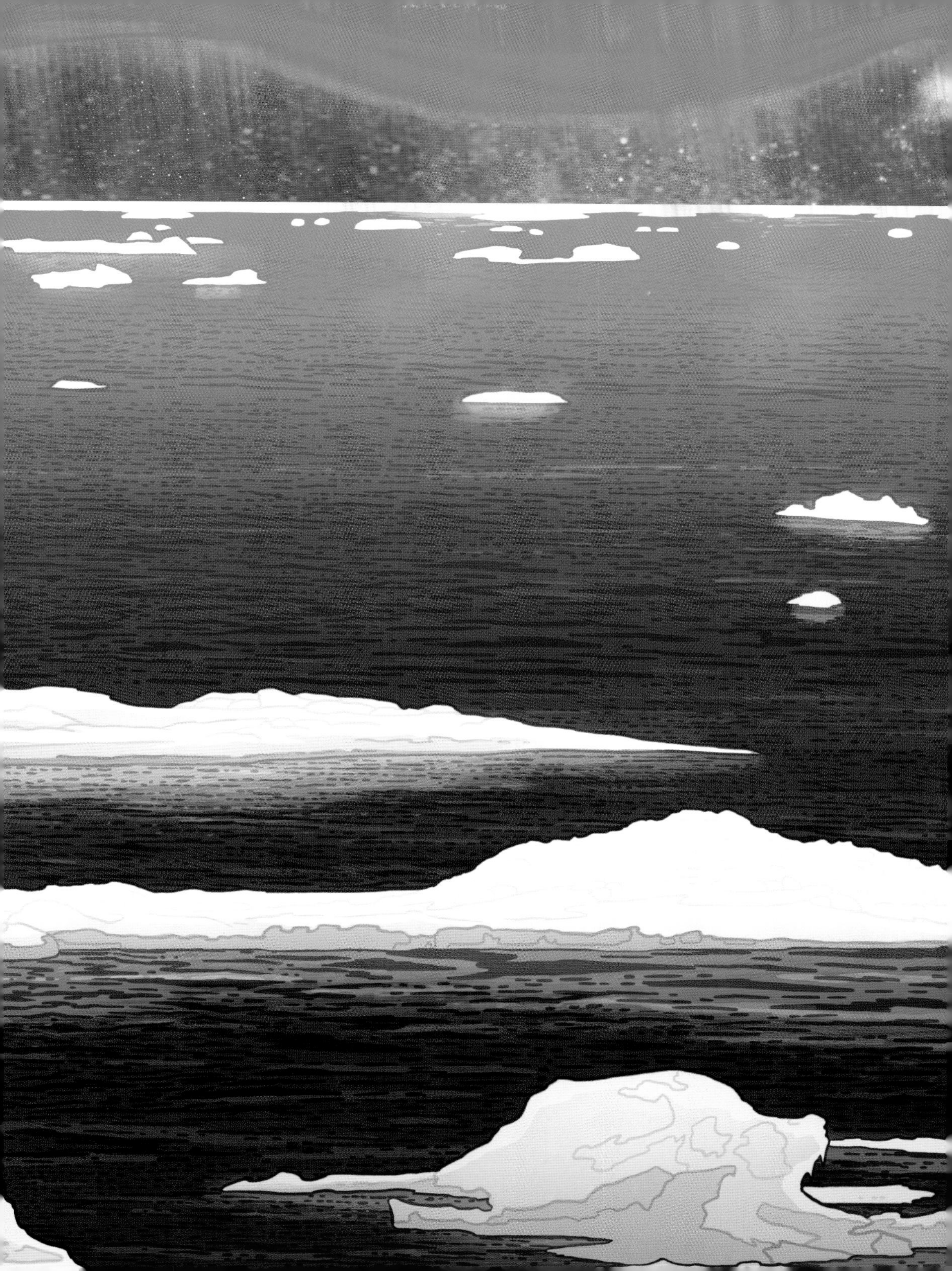

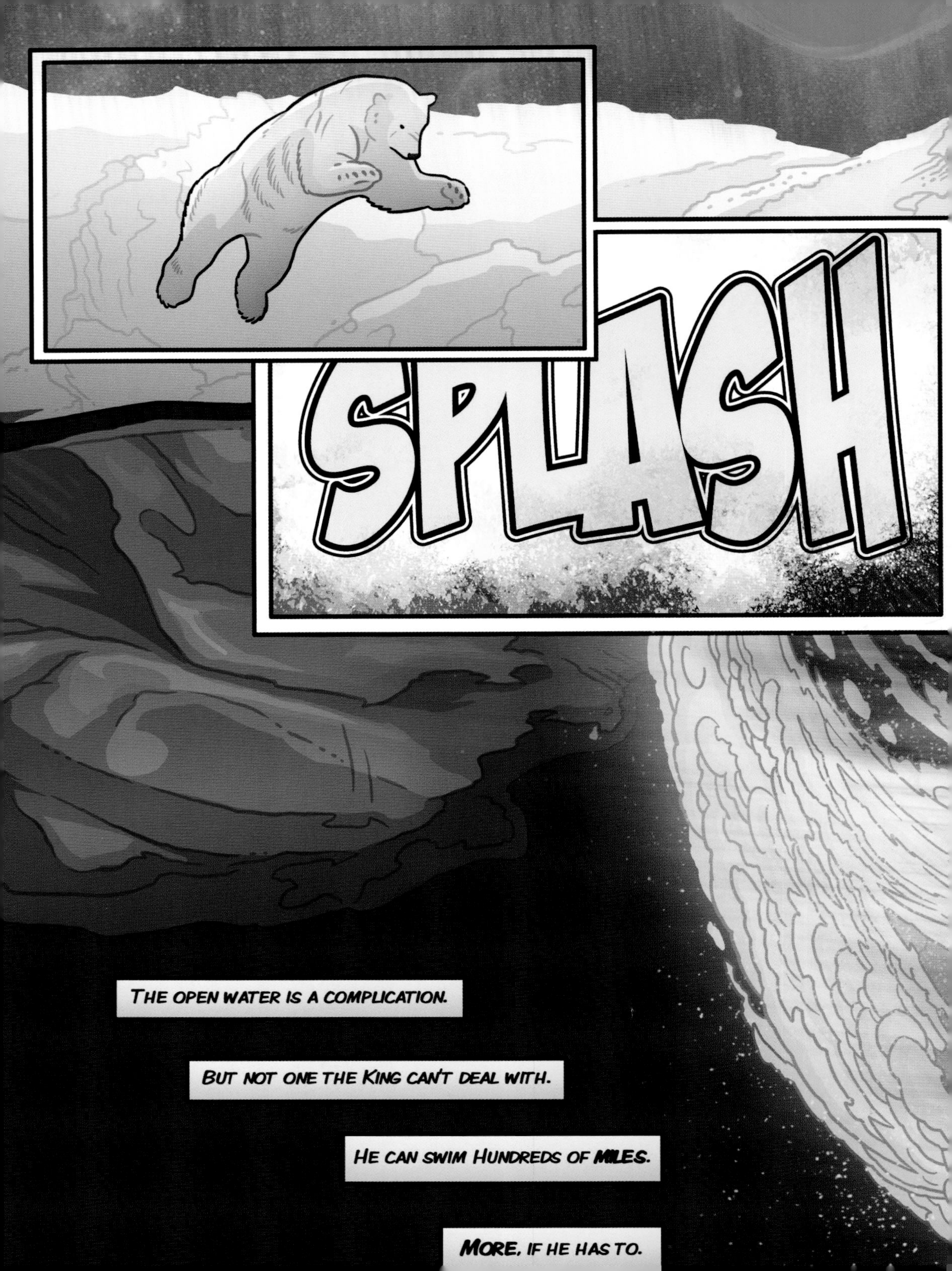
SPLASH
THE OPEN WATER IS A COMPLICATION.
BUT NOT ONE THE KING CAN'T DEAL WITH.
HE CAN SWIM HUNDREDS OF MILES.
MORE, IF HE HAS TO.

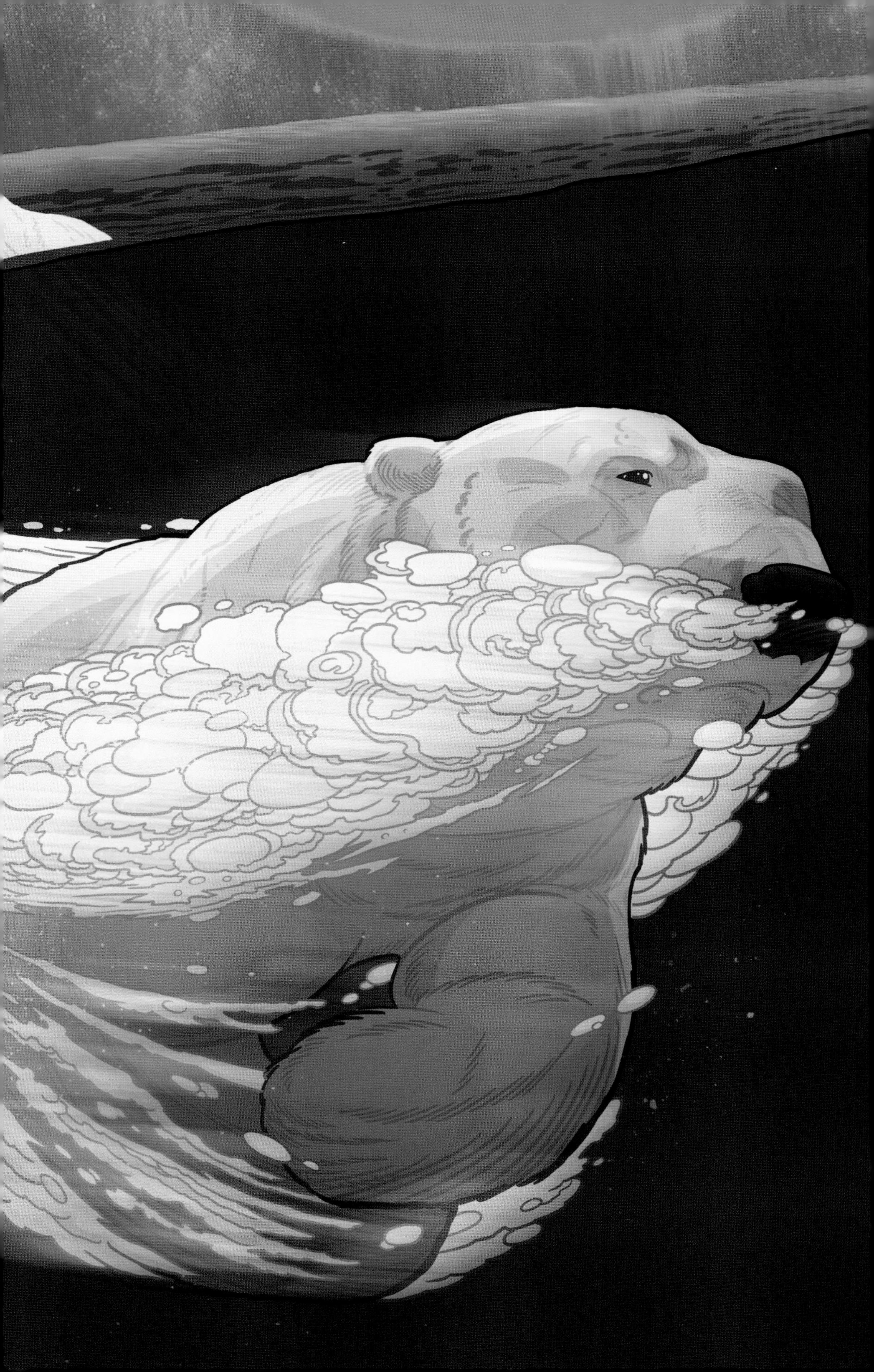

POLAR BEARS ARE EQUALLY AT HOME IN THE WATER AS THEY ARE ON THE ICE.

BUT THIS BEAR'S **MARATHON** SWIM WILL HAVE BEEN FOR **NOTHING** IF HE CAN'T PICK UP THE SCENT TRAIL AGAIN.

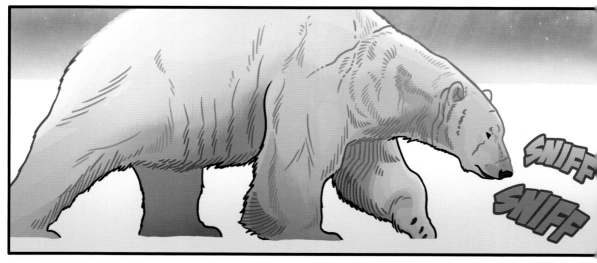

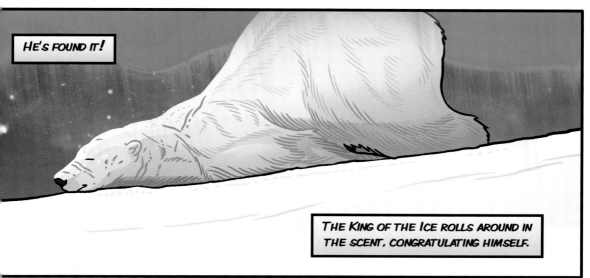

HE'S FOUND IT!

THE KING OF THE ICE ROLLS AROUND IN THE SCENT, CONGRATULATING HIMSELF.

THE TRAIL IS STRONG.

NOT FAR TO GO NOW.

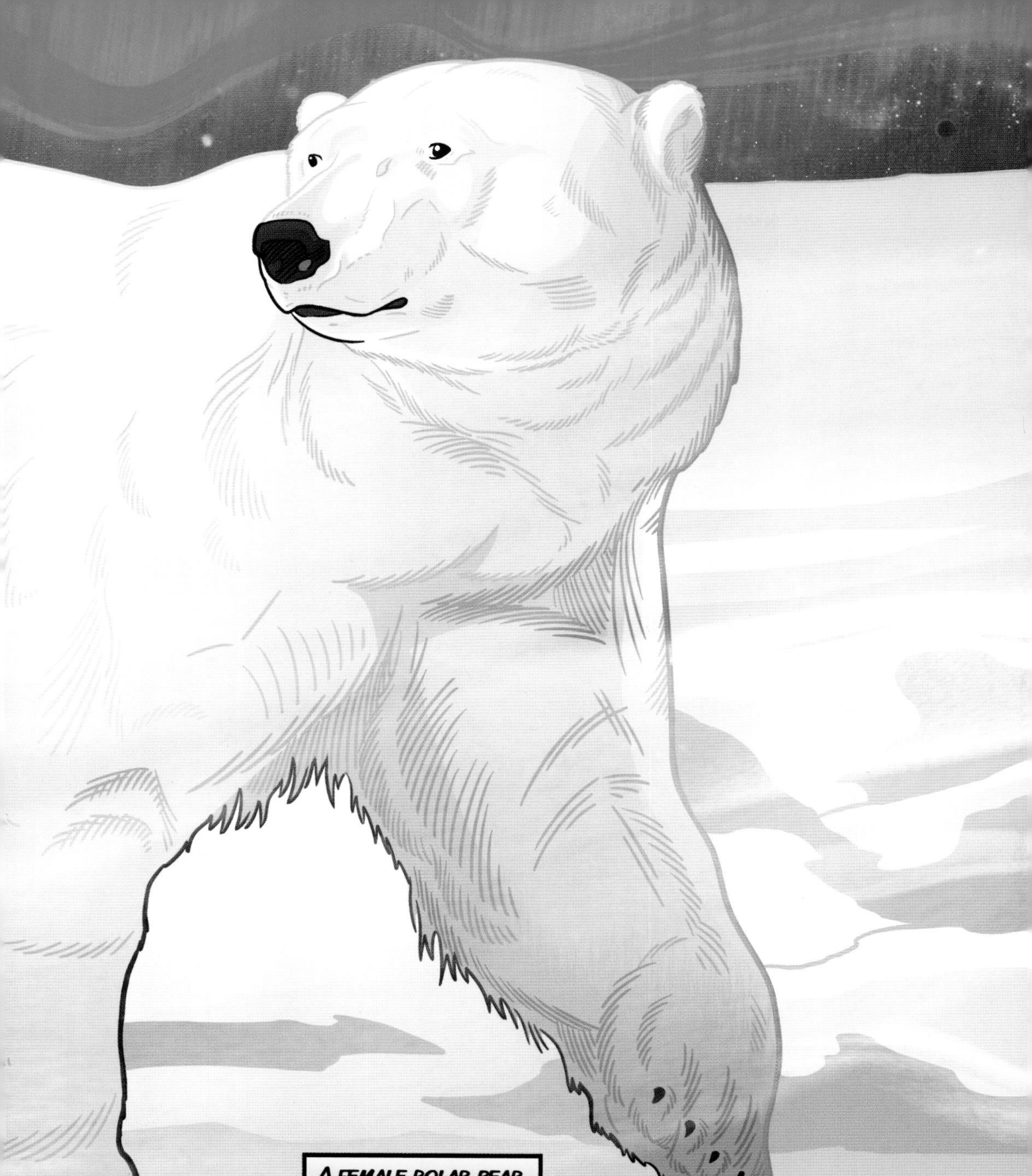
A FEMALE POLAR BEAR.

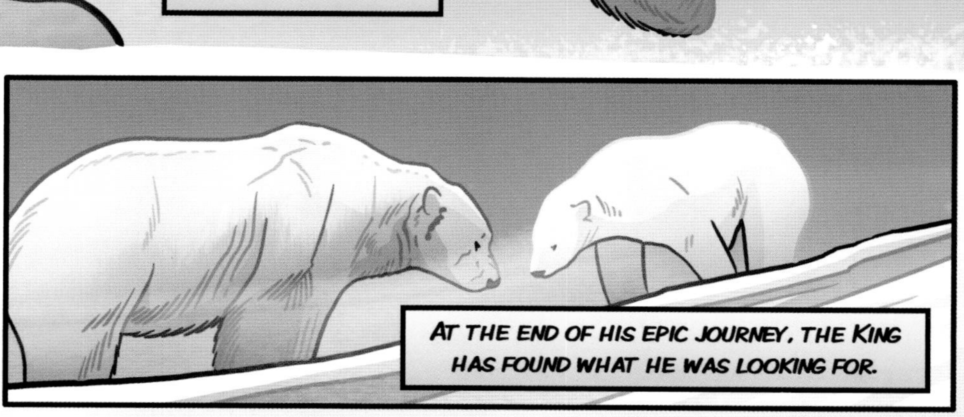
AT THE END OF HIS EPIC JOURNEY, THE KING HAS FOUND WHAT HE WAS LOOKING FOR.

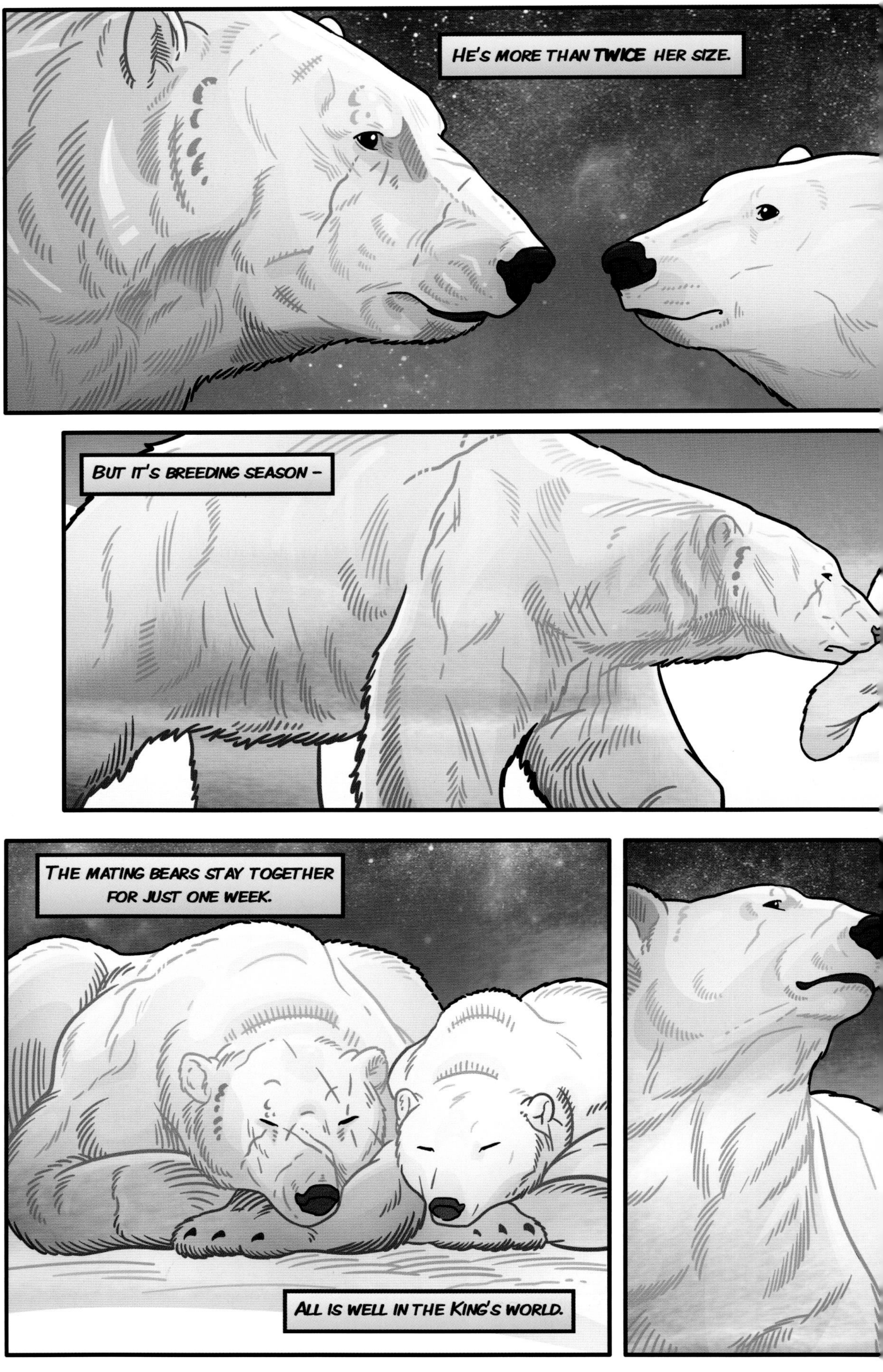
HE'S MORE THAN TWICE HER SIZE.
BUT IT'S BREEDING SEASON -
THE MATING BEARS STAY TOGETHER FOR JUST ONE WEEK.
ALL IS WELL IN THE KING'S WORLD.

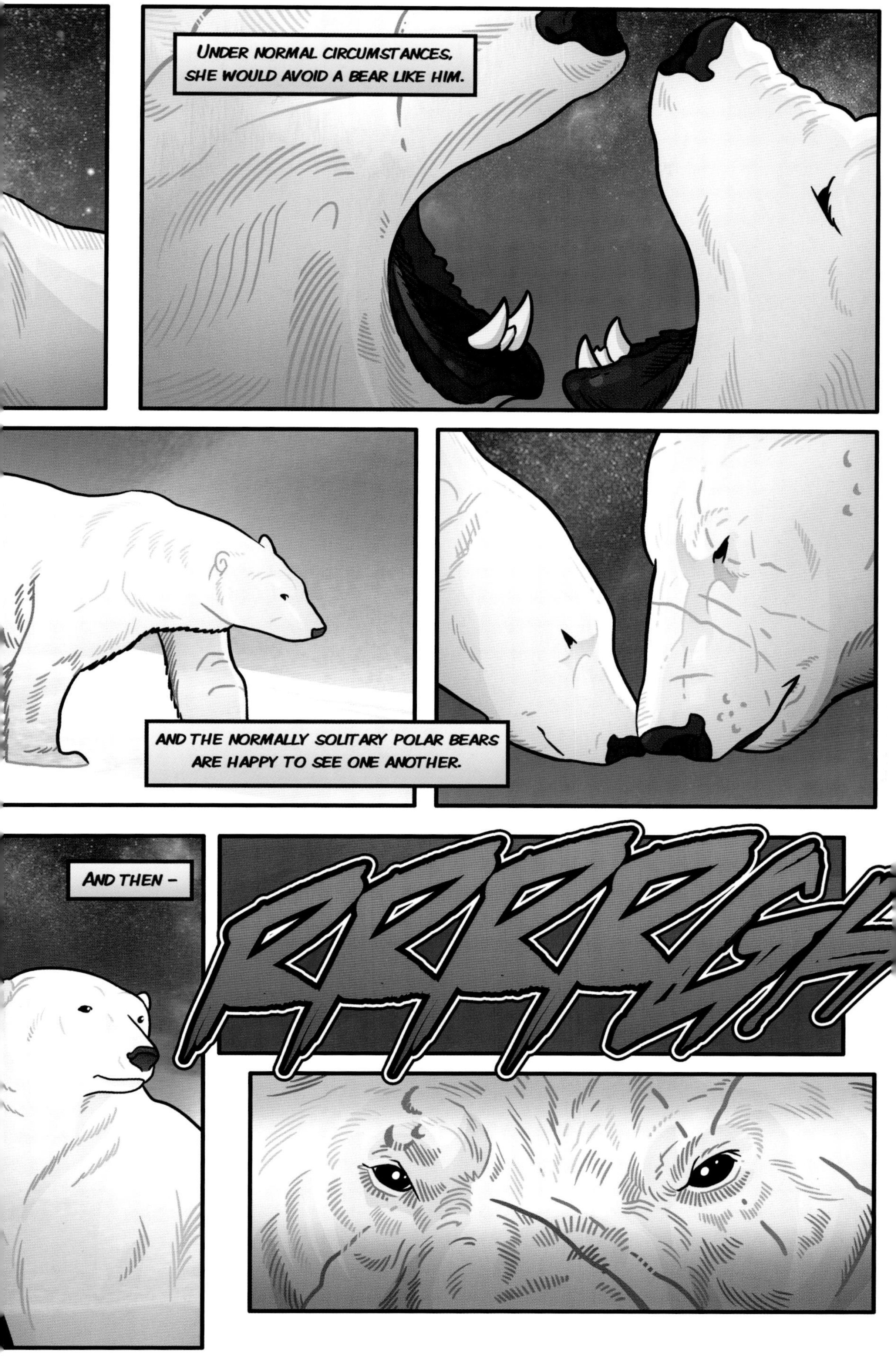
UNDER NORMAL CIRCUMSTANCES, SHE WOULD AVOID A BEAR LIKE HIM.
AND THE NORMALLY SOLITARY POLAR BEARS ARE HAPPY TO SEE ONE ANOTHER.
AND THEN -
RRRRGH

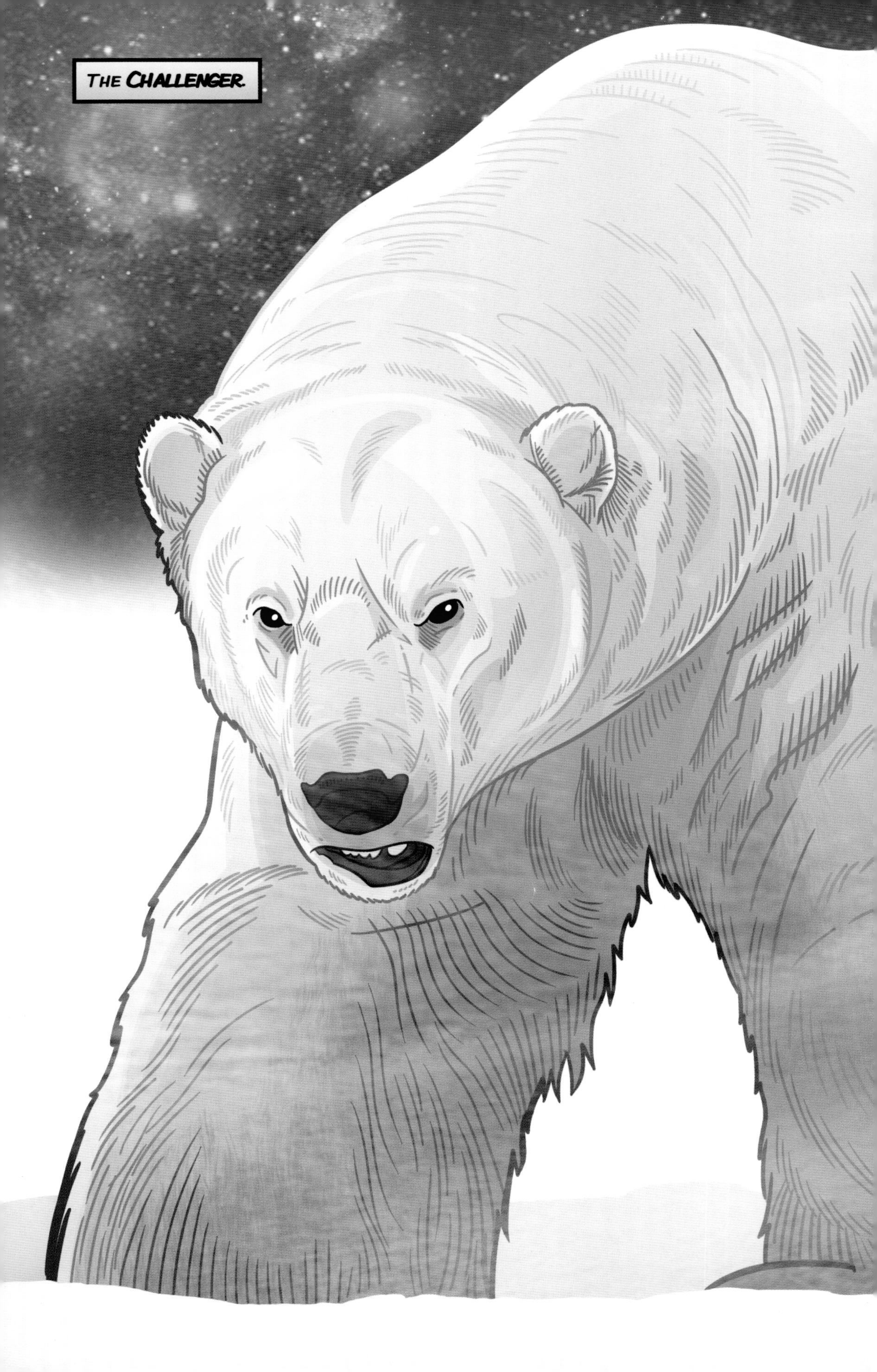
THE CHALLENGER.

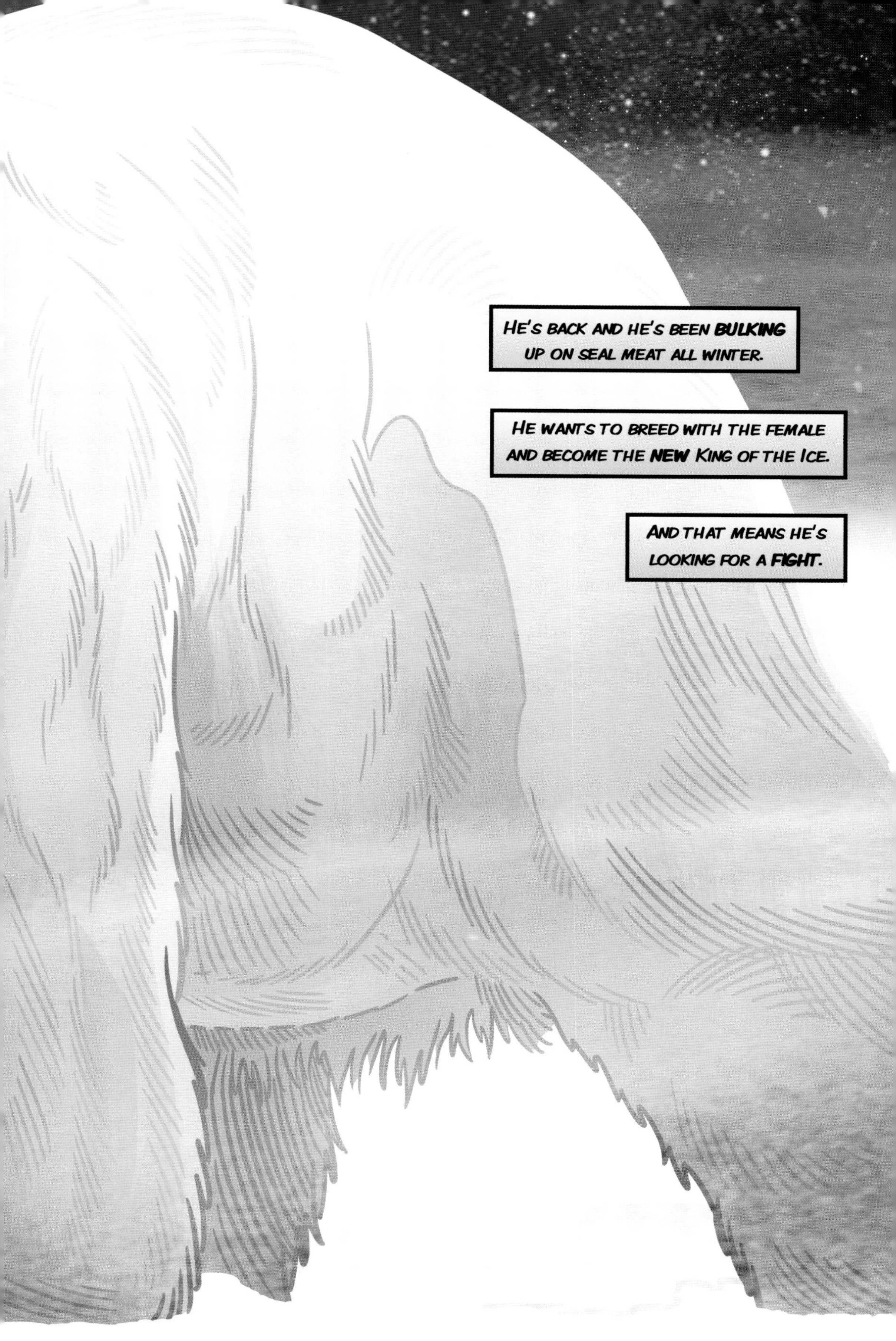
HE'S BACK AND HE'S BEEN BULKING UP ON SEAL MEAT ALL WINTER.
HE WANTS TO BREED WITH THE FEMALE AND BECOME THE NEW KING OF THE ICE.
AND THAT MEANS HE'S LOOKING FOR A FIGHT.

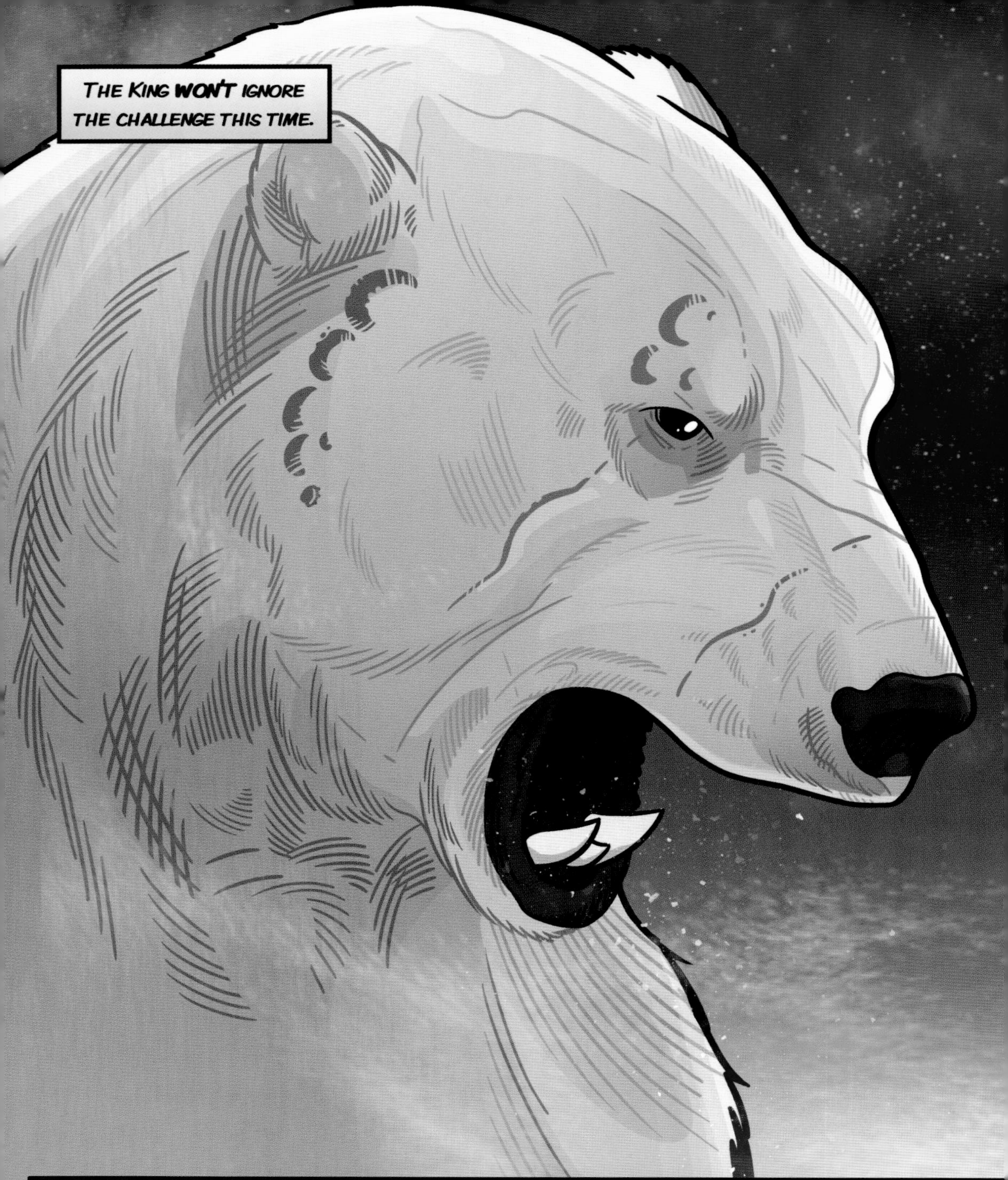
THE KING WON'T IGNORE THE CHALLENGE THIS TIME.

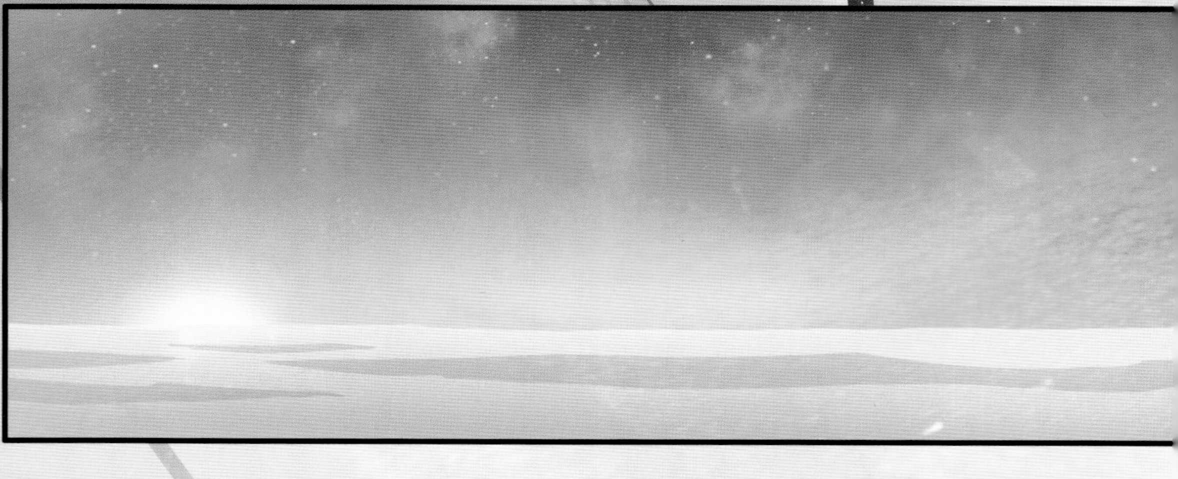

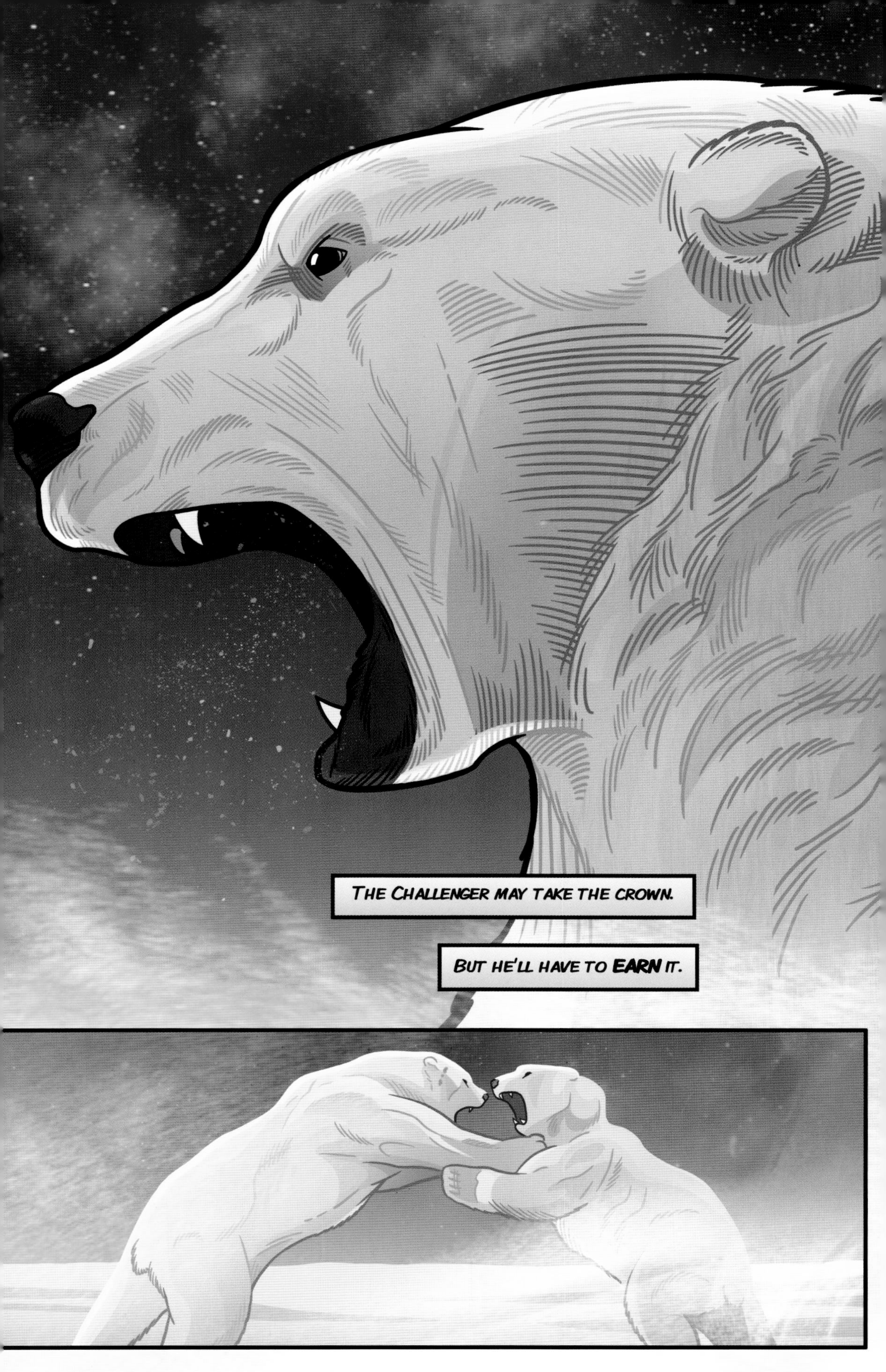
THE CHALLENGER MAY TAKE THE CROWN.
BUT HE'LL HAVE TO EARN IT.

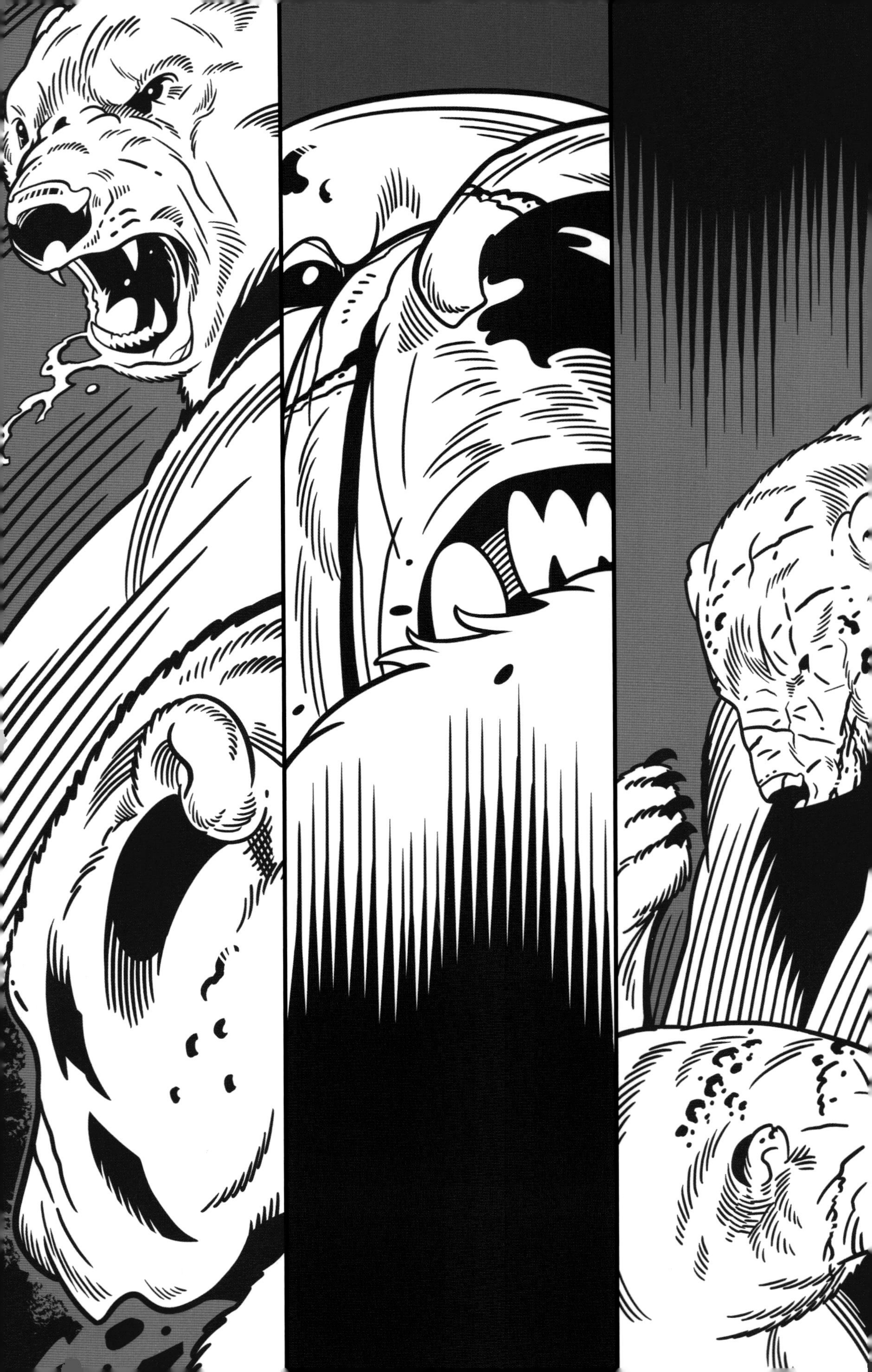

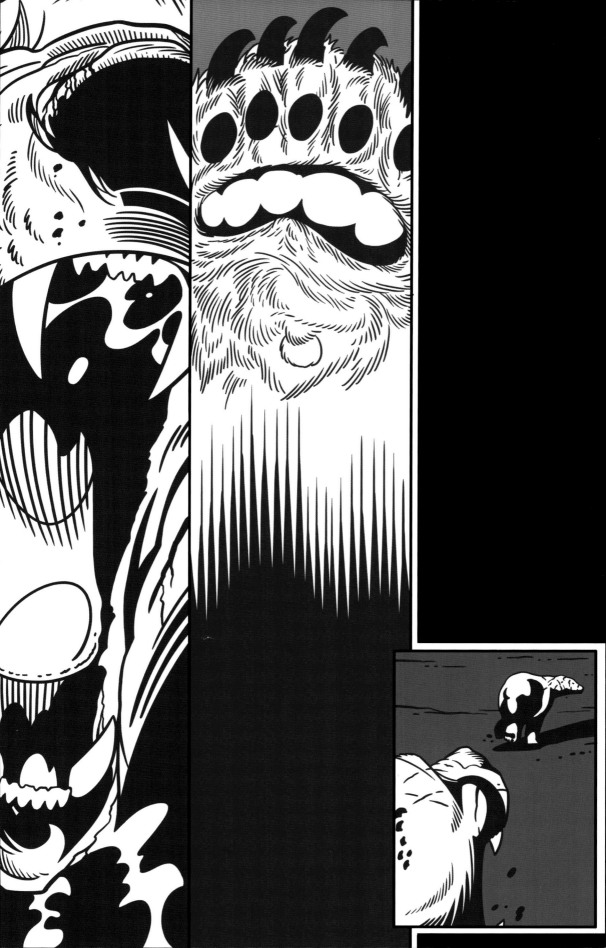

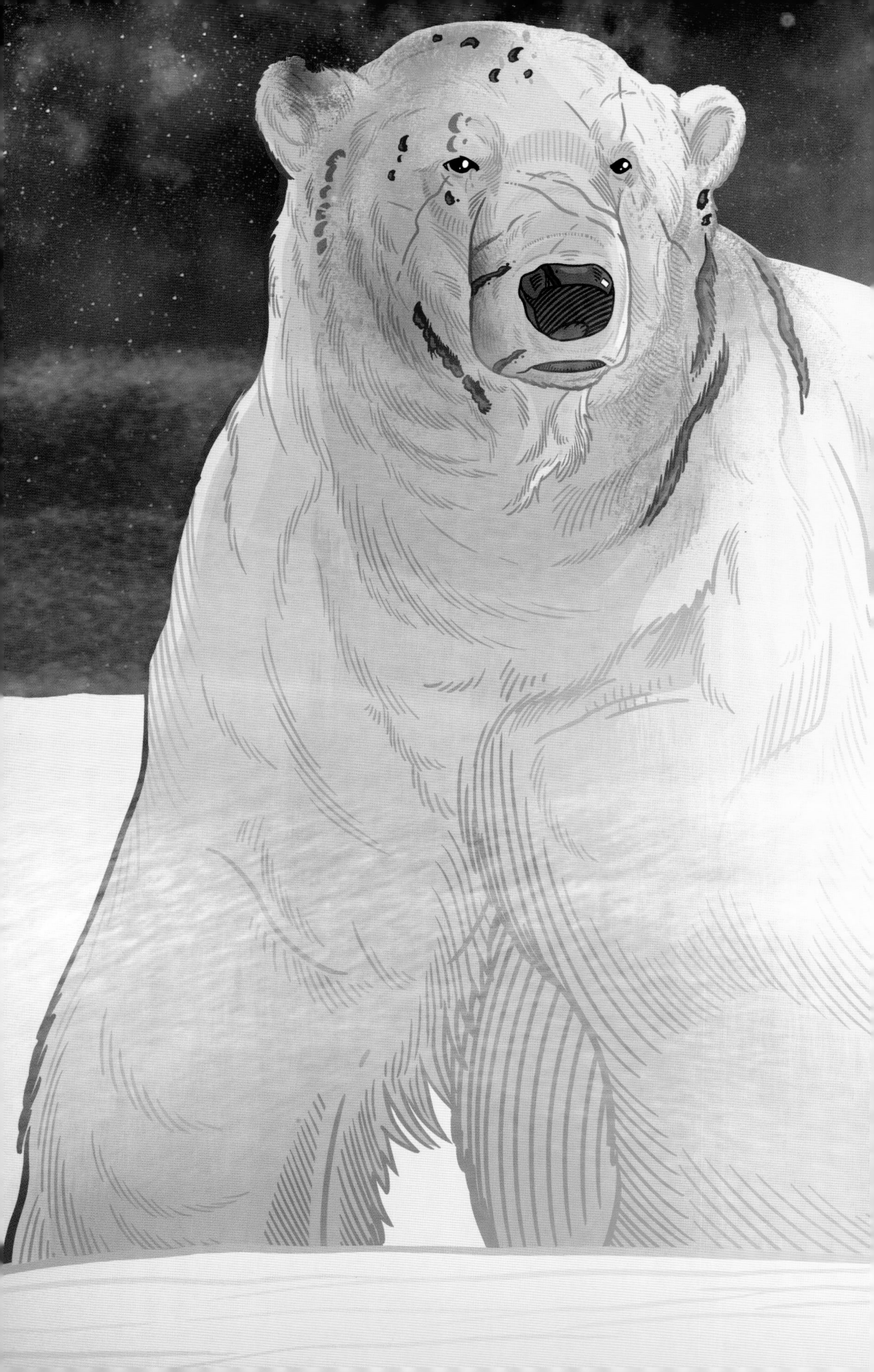

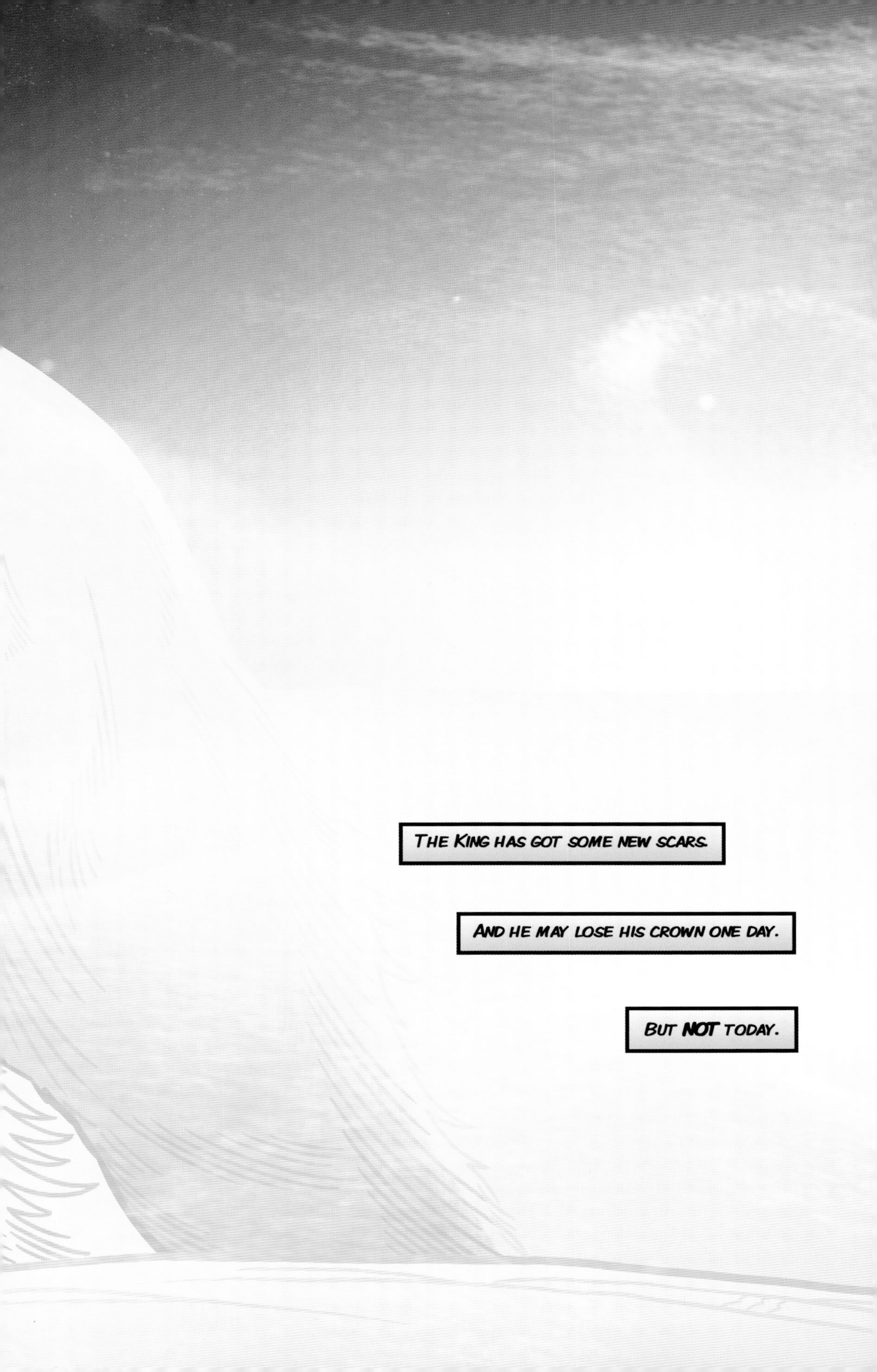
THE KING HAS GOT SOME NEW SCARS.
AND HE MAY LOSE HIS CROWN ONE DAY.
BUT NOT TODAY.

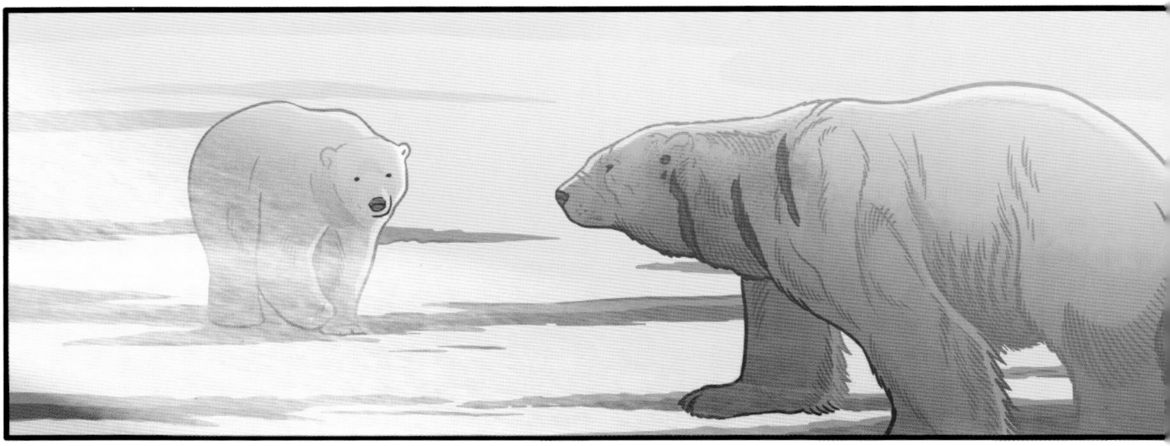

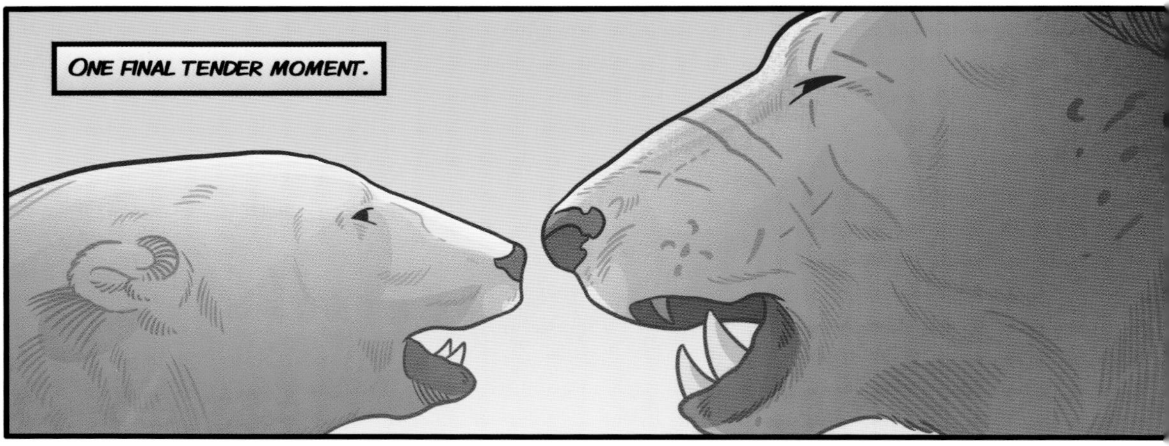
ONE FINAL TENDER MOMENT.

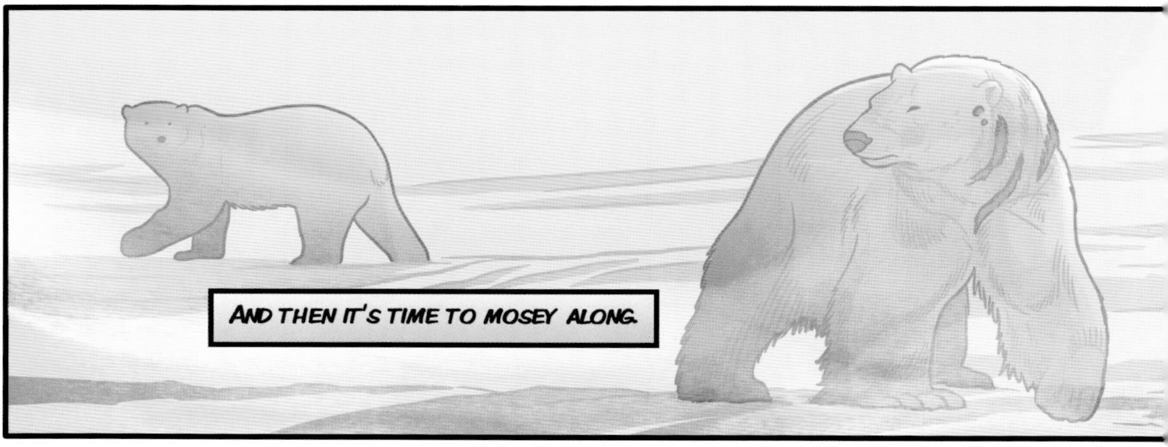
AND THEN IT'S TIME TO MOSEY ALONG.

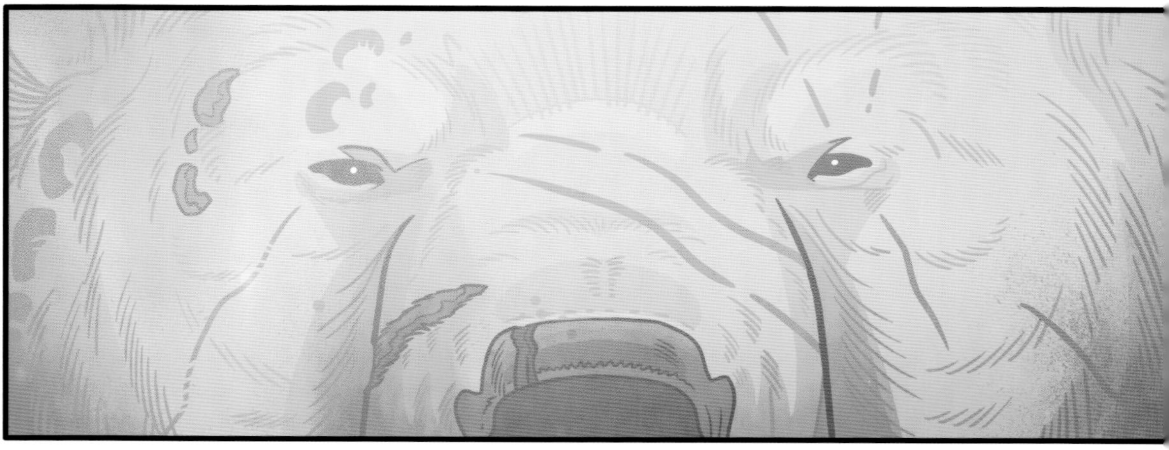

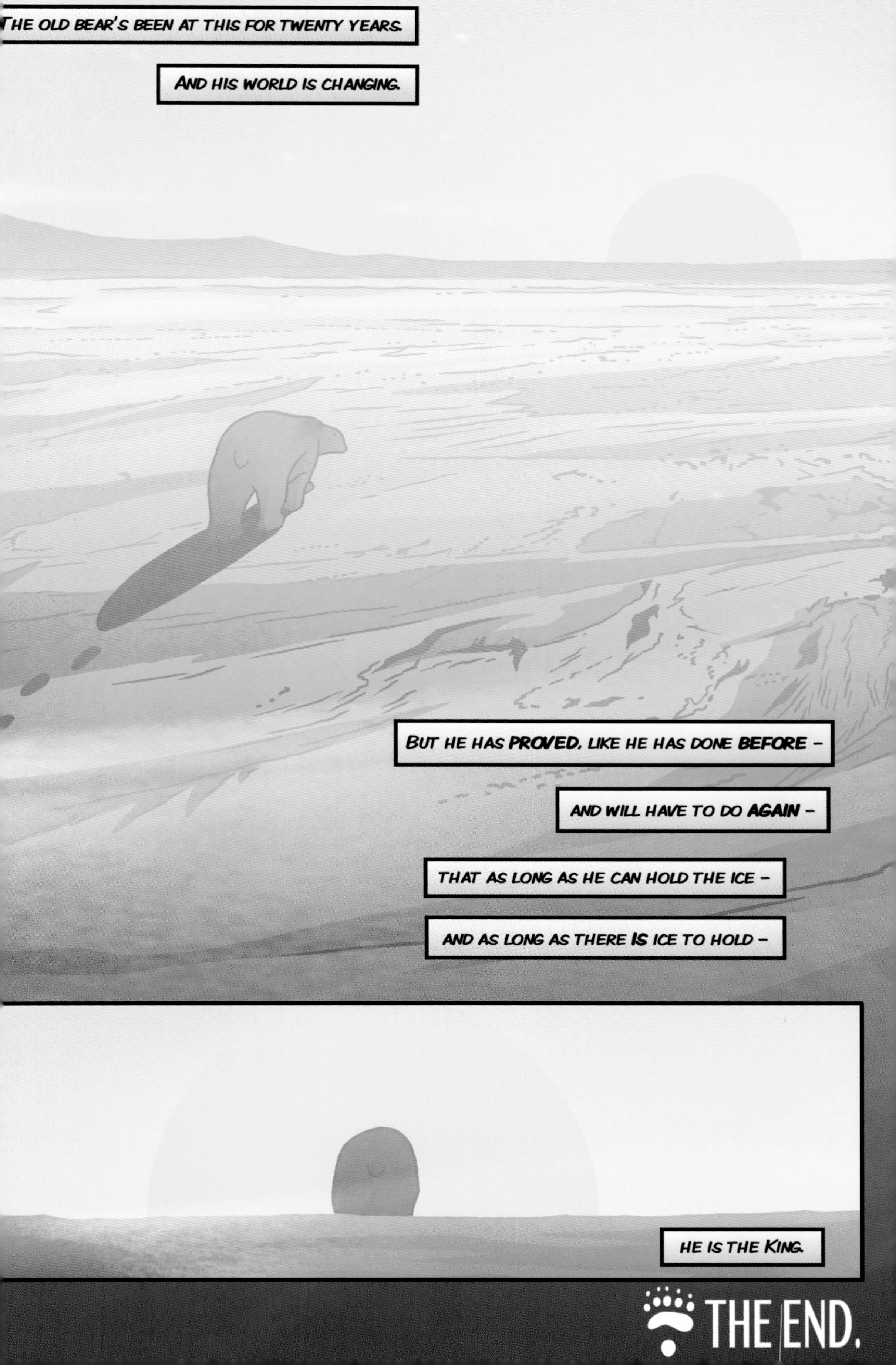
THE OLD BEAR'S BEEN AT THIS FOR TWENTY YEARS.
AND HIS WORLD IS CHANGING.
BUT HE HAS **PROVED**, LIKE HE HAS DONE **BEFORE** –
AND WILL HAVE TO DO **AGAIN** –
THAT AS LONG AS HE CAN HOLD THE ICE –
AND AS LONG AS THERE **IS** ICE TO HOLD –
HE IS THE KING.
THE END.

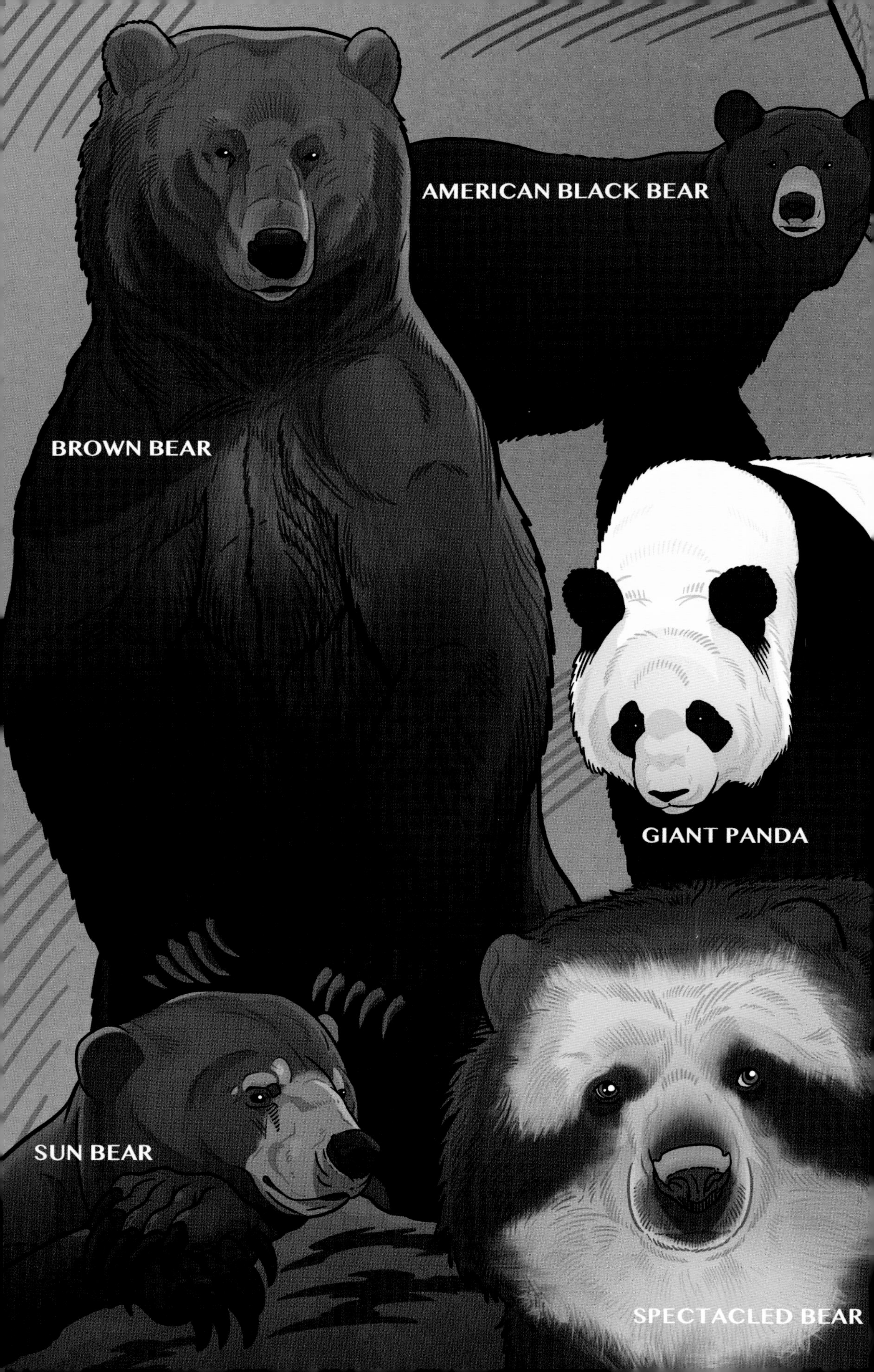
AMERICAN BLACK BEAR
BROWN BEAR
GIANT PANDA
SUN BEAR
SPECTACLED BEAR

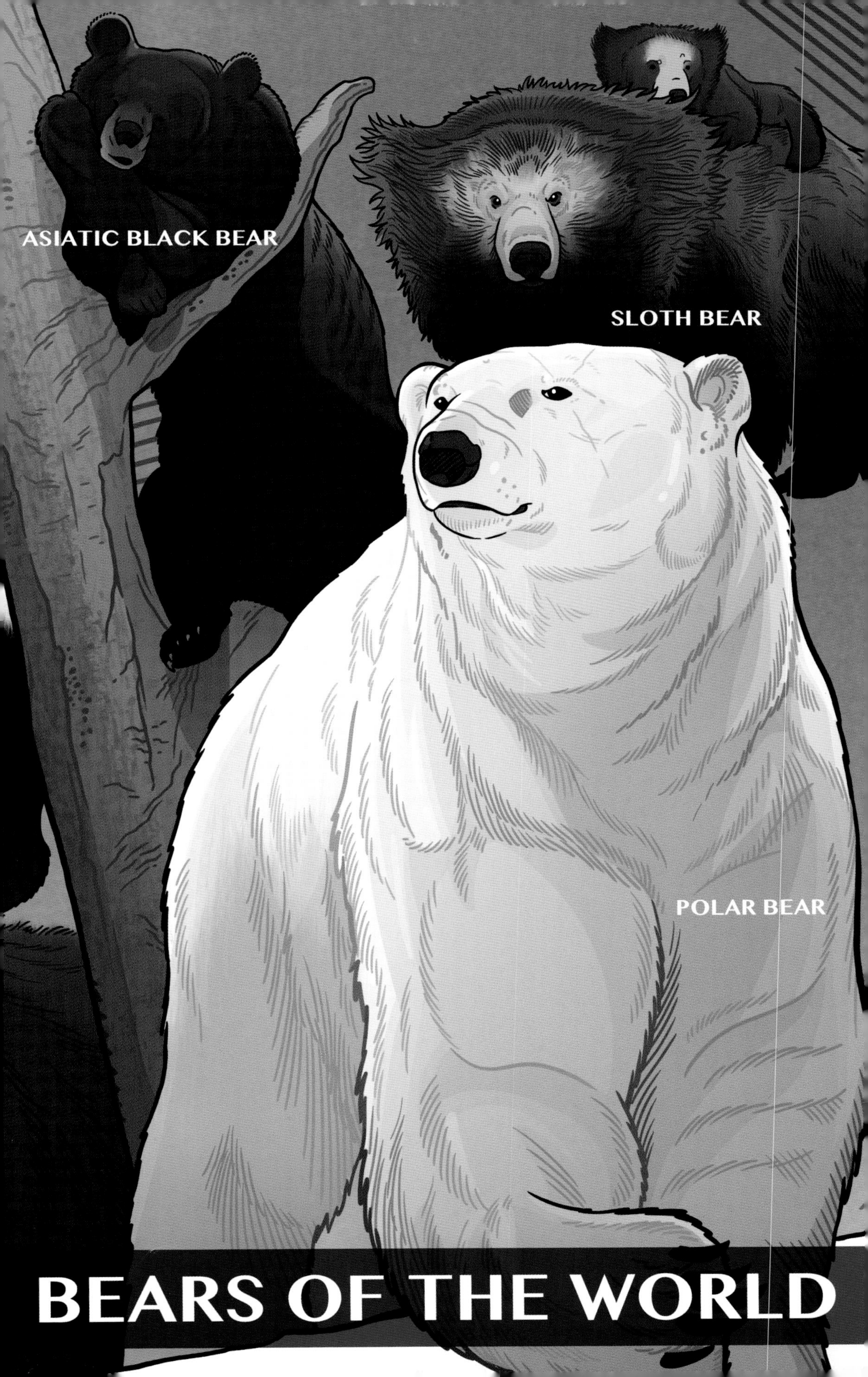
ASIATIC BLACK BEAR
SLOTH BEAR
POLAR BEAR
BEARS OF THE WORLD

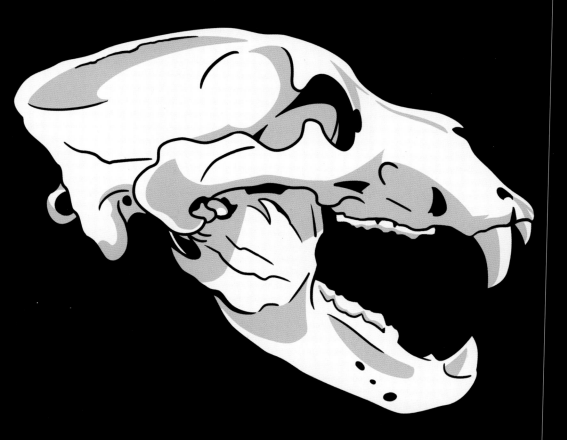

REXTOOTH
STUDIOS
REXTOOTH.COM

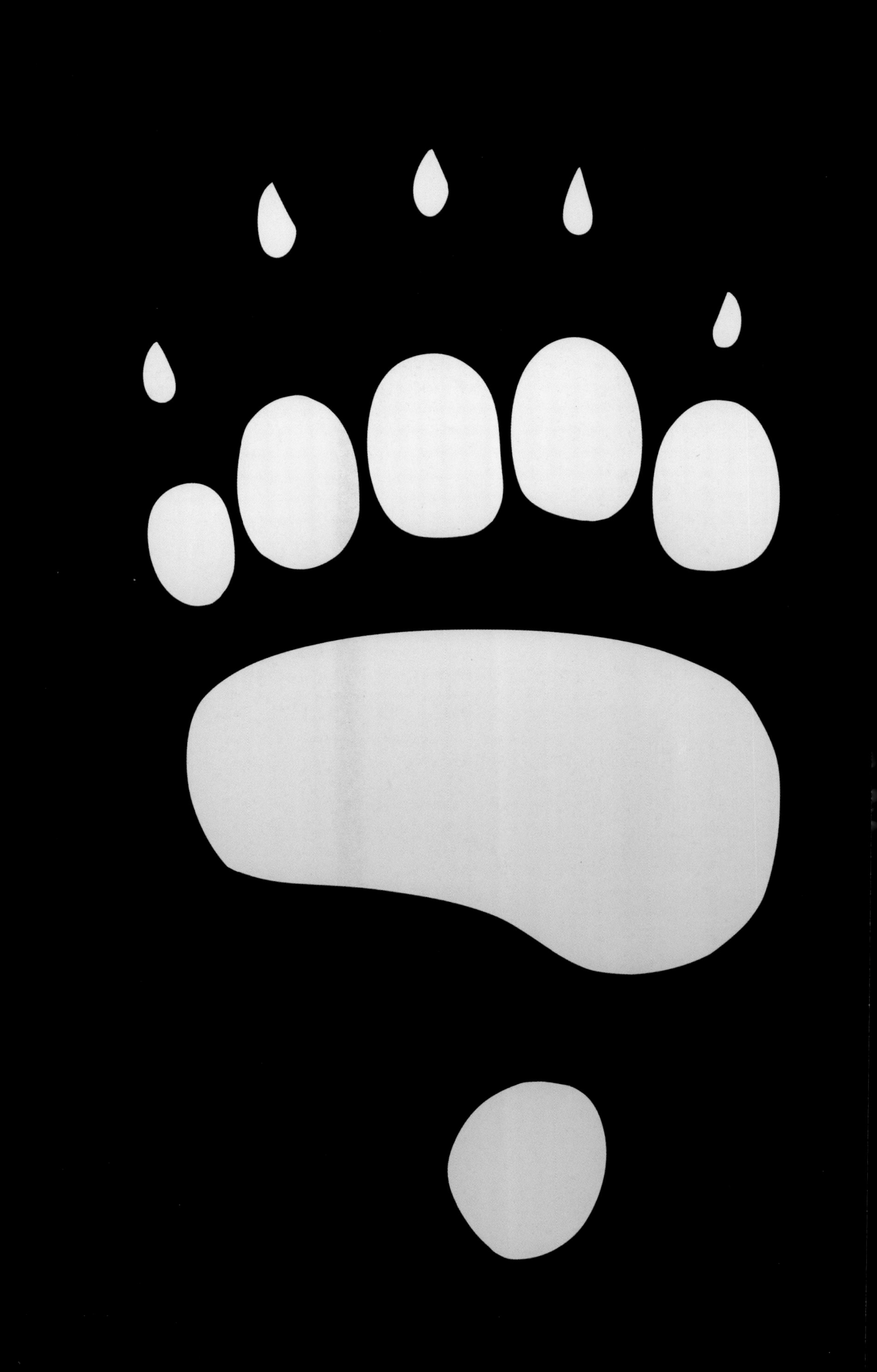